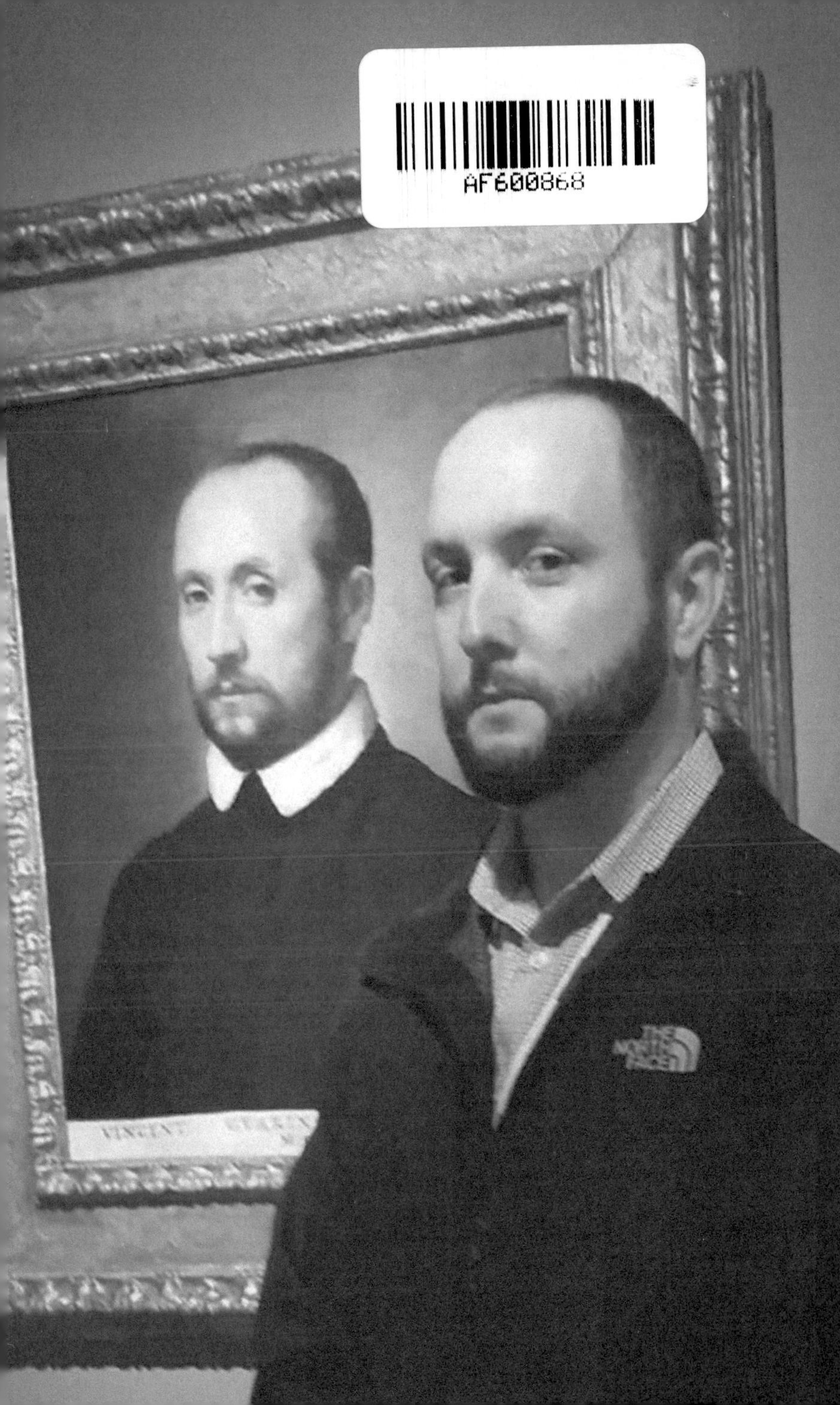
THE NORTH FACE

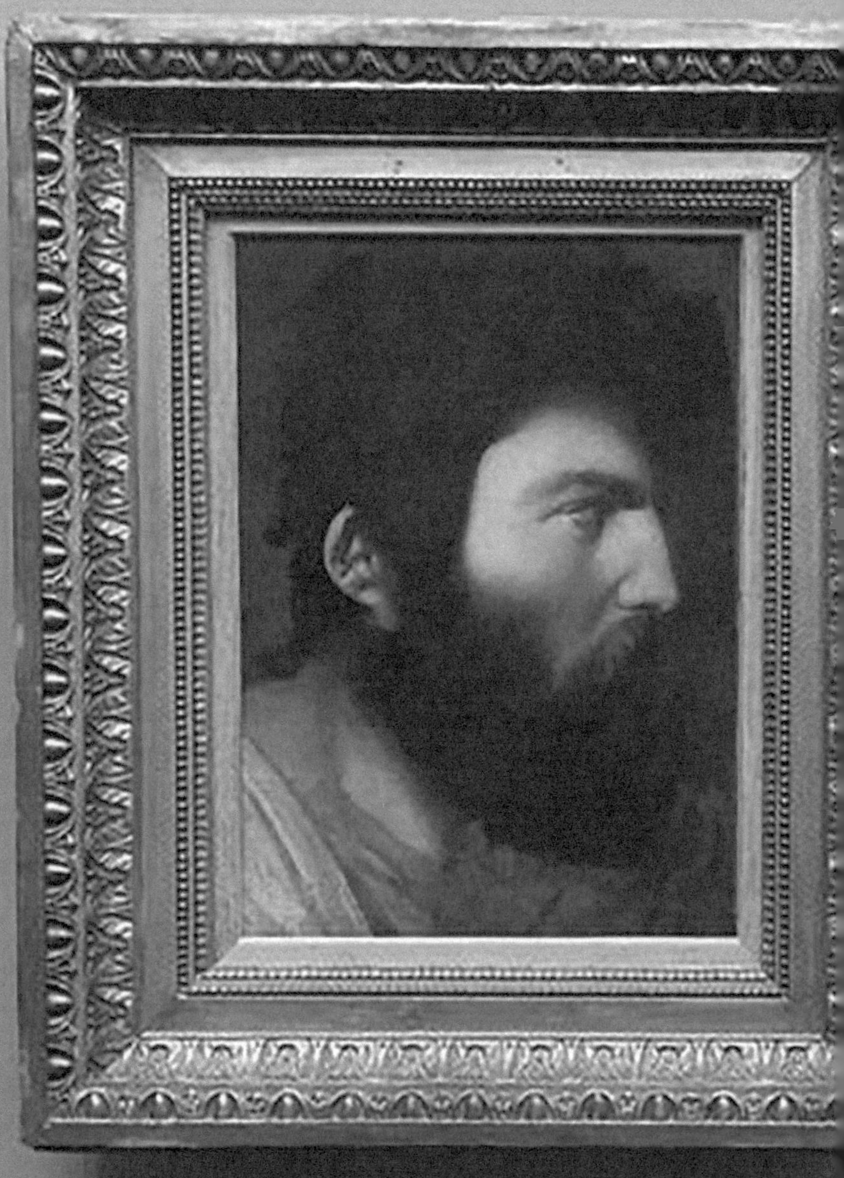

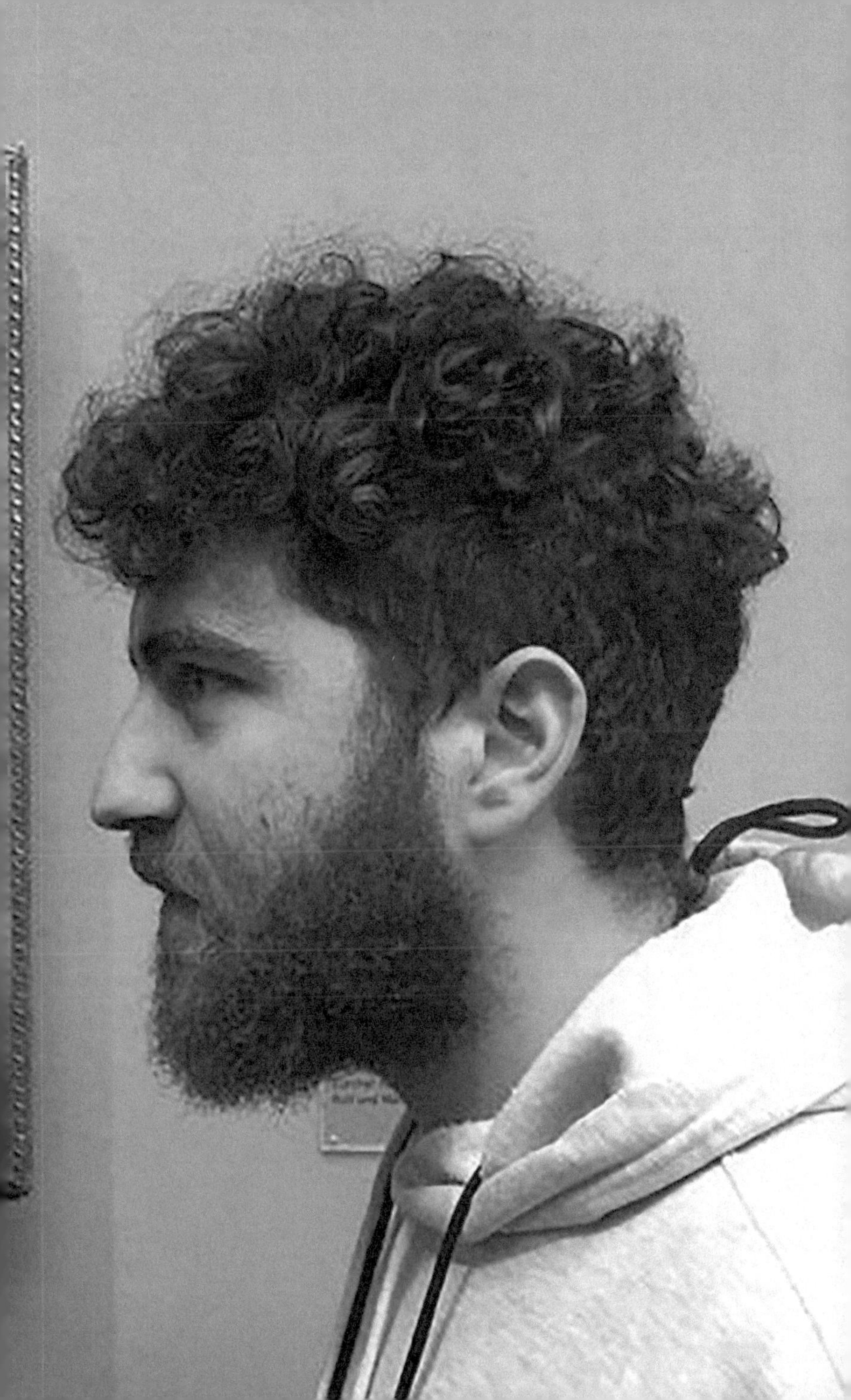

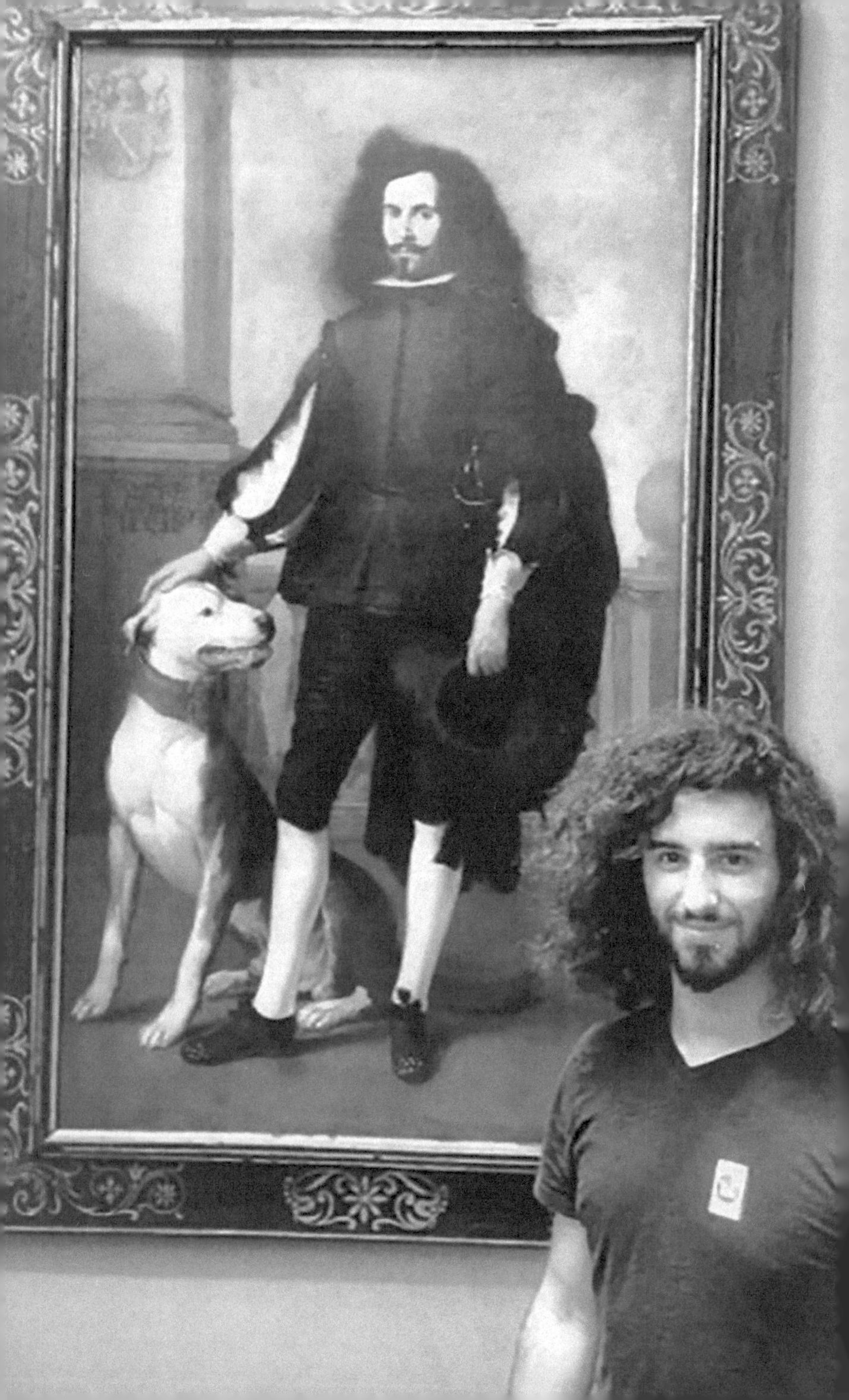

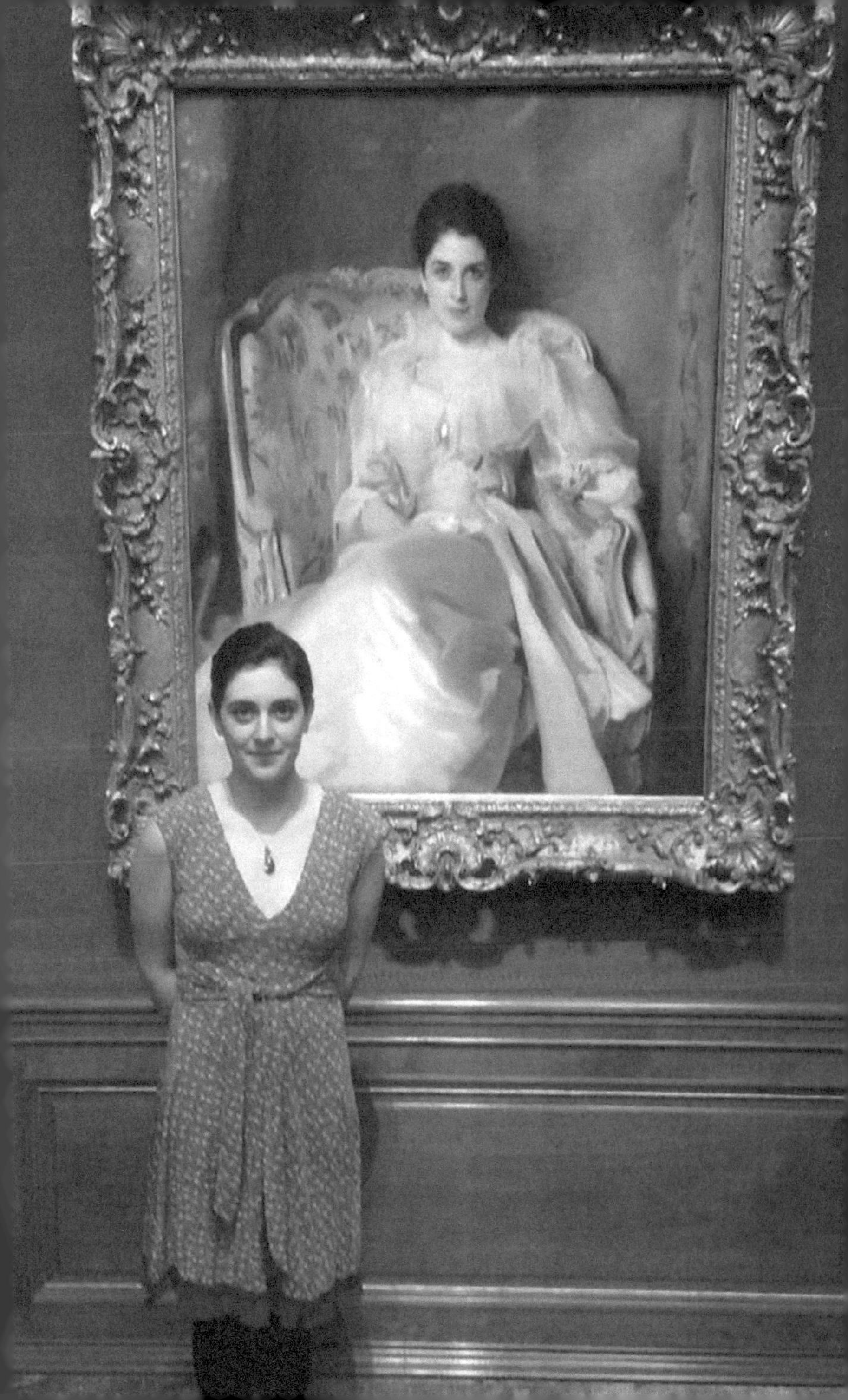

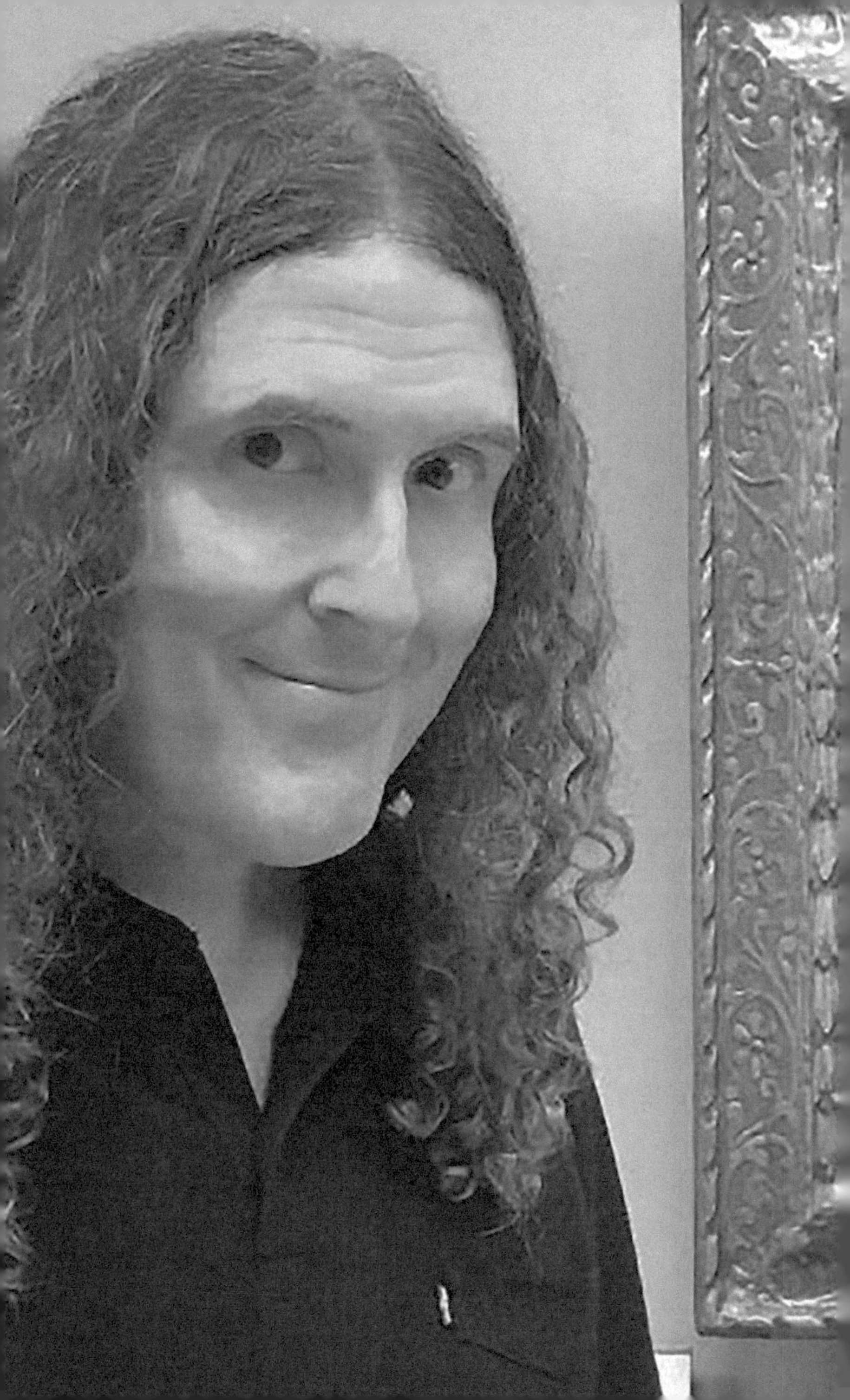

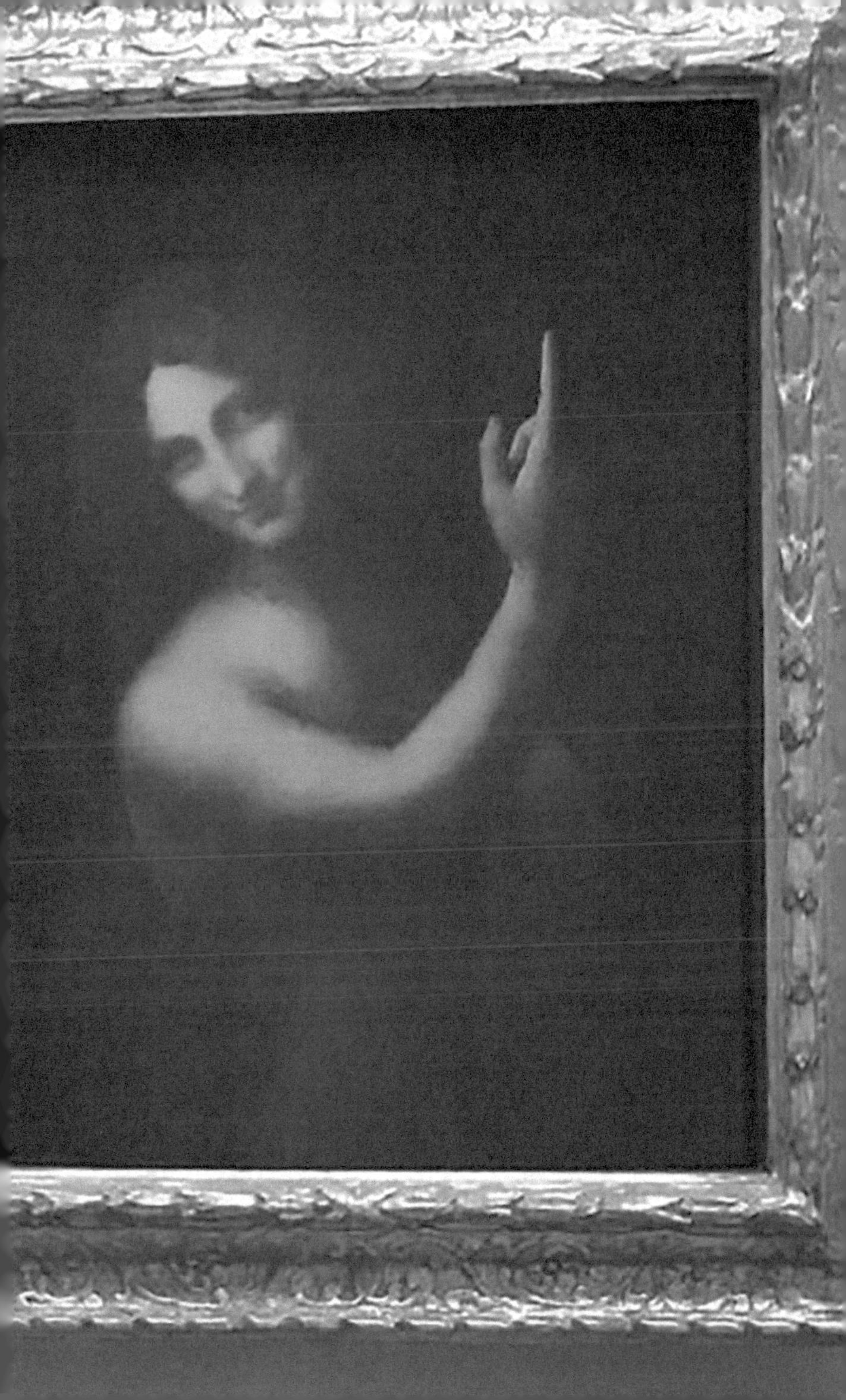

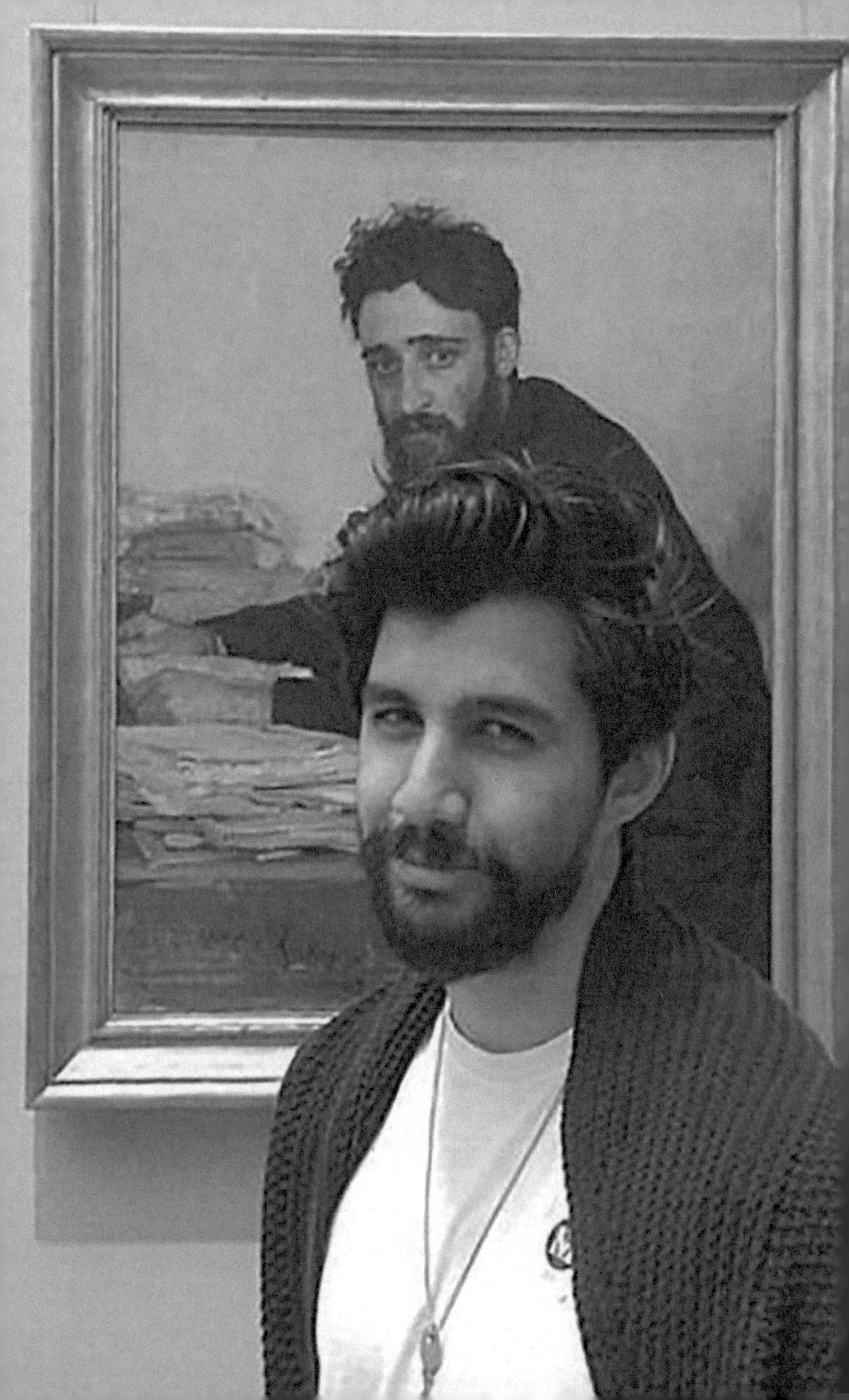

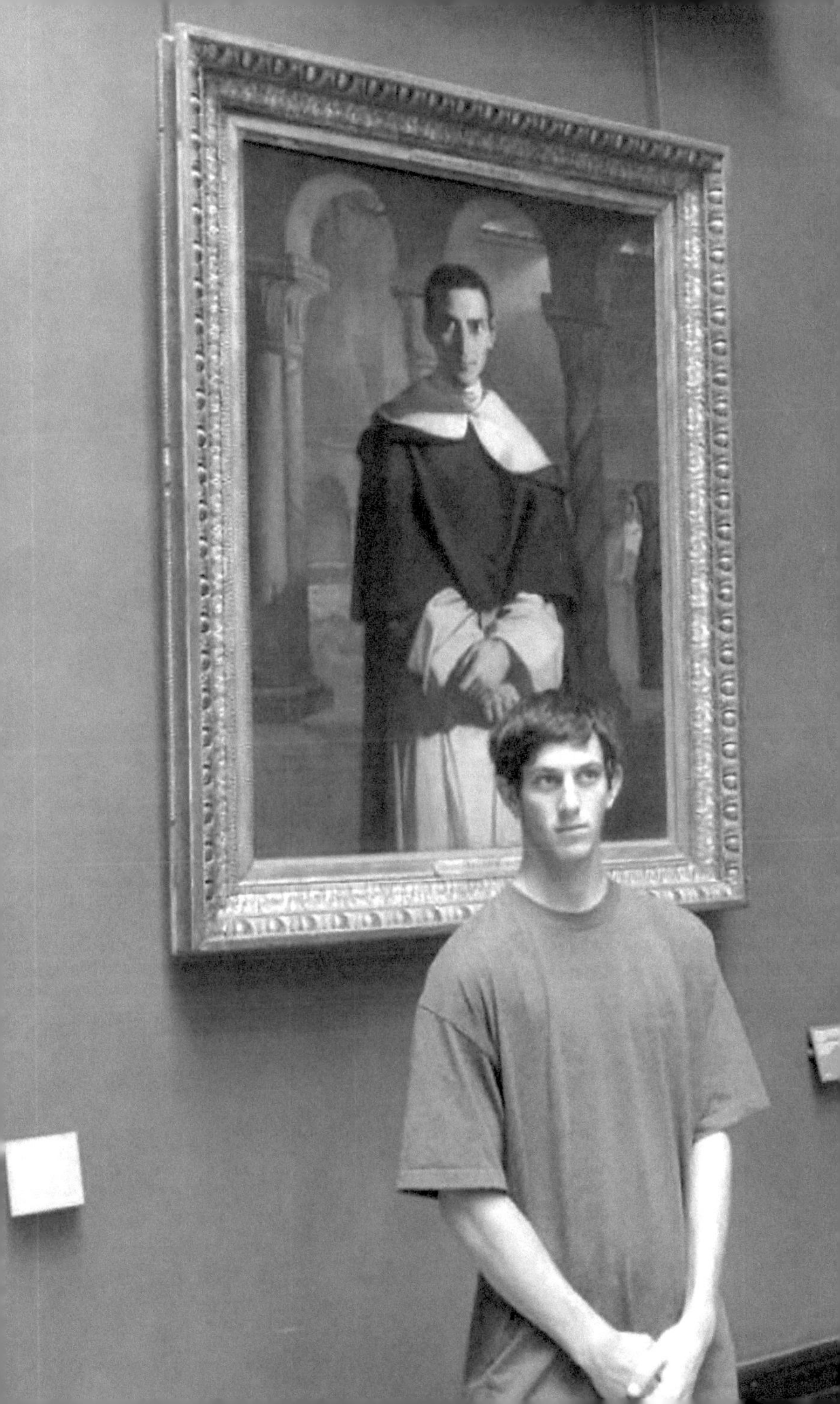

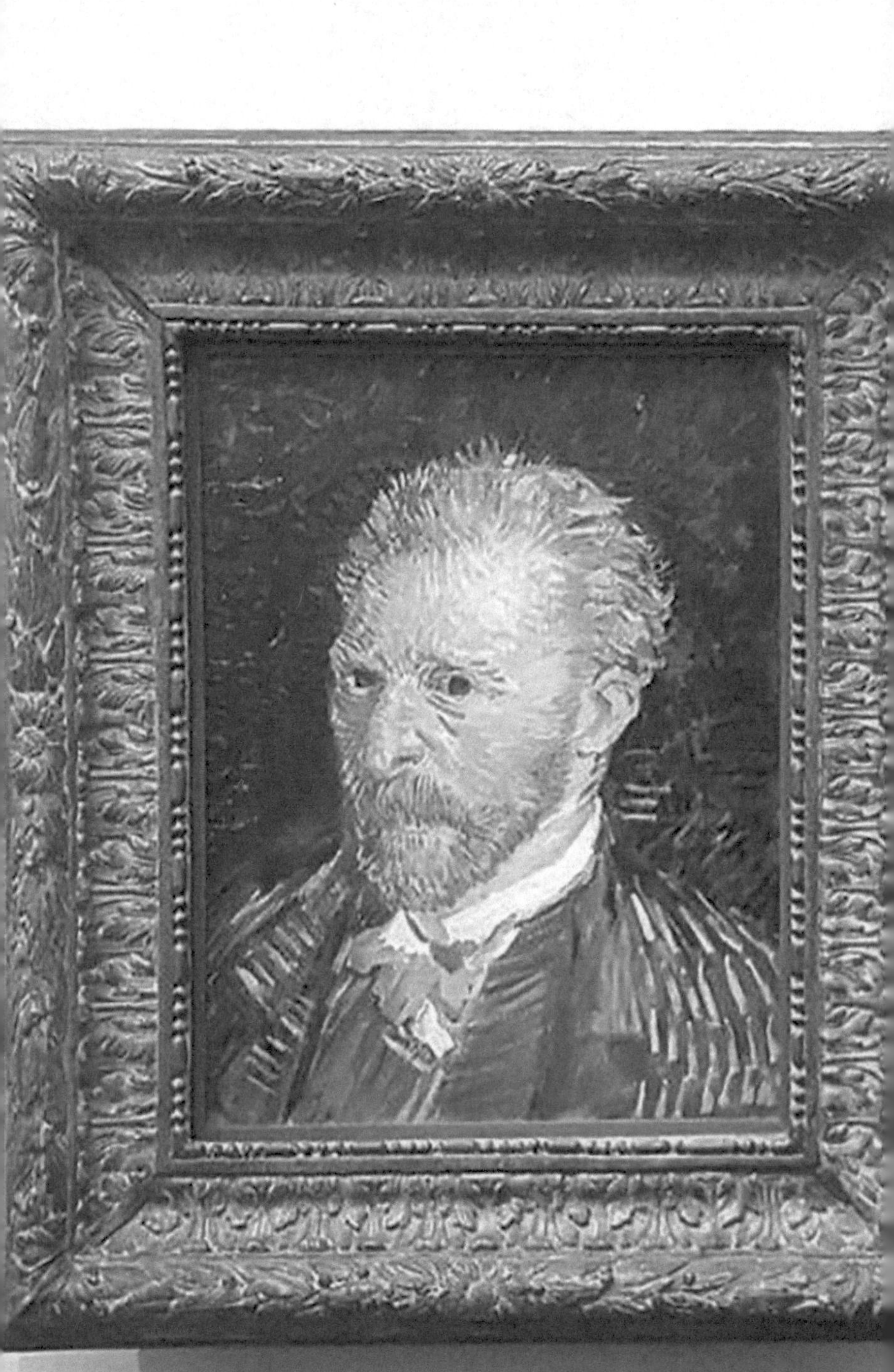

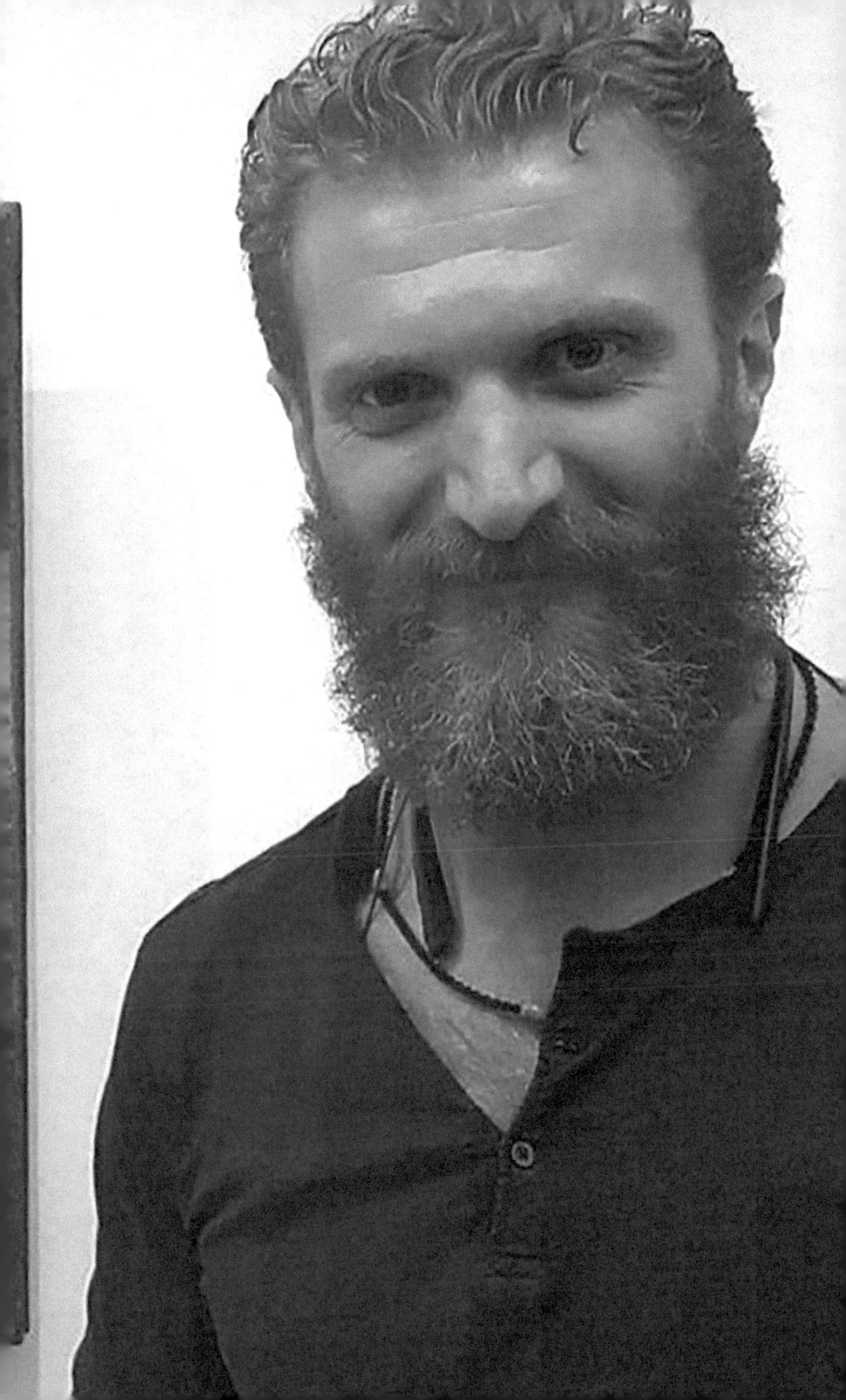

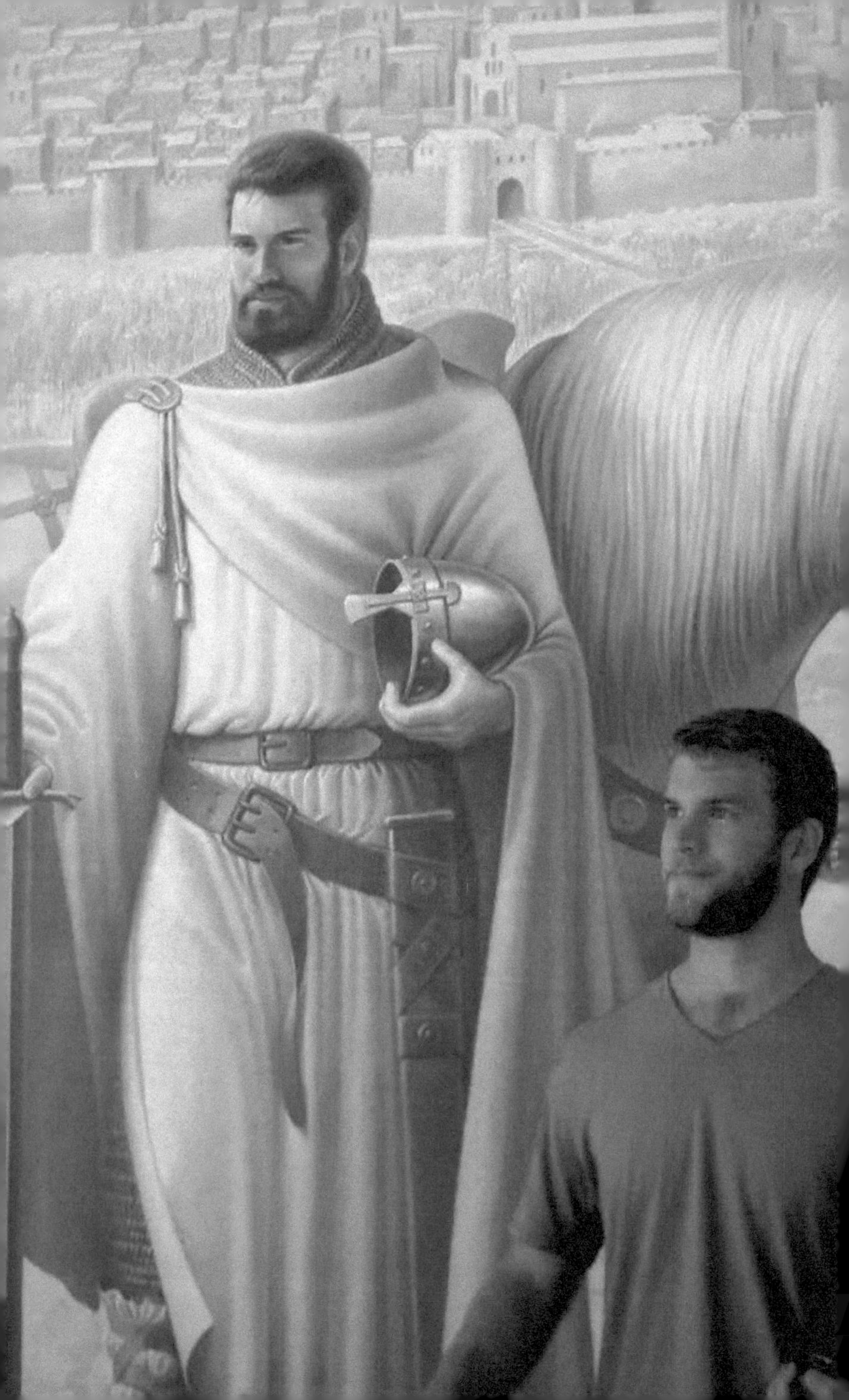

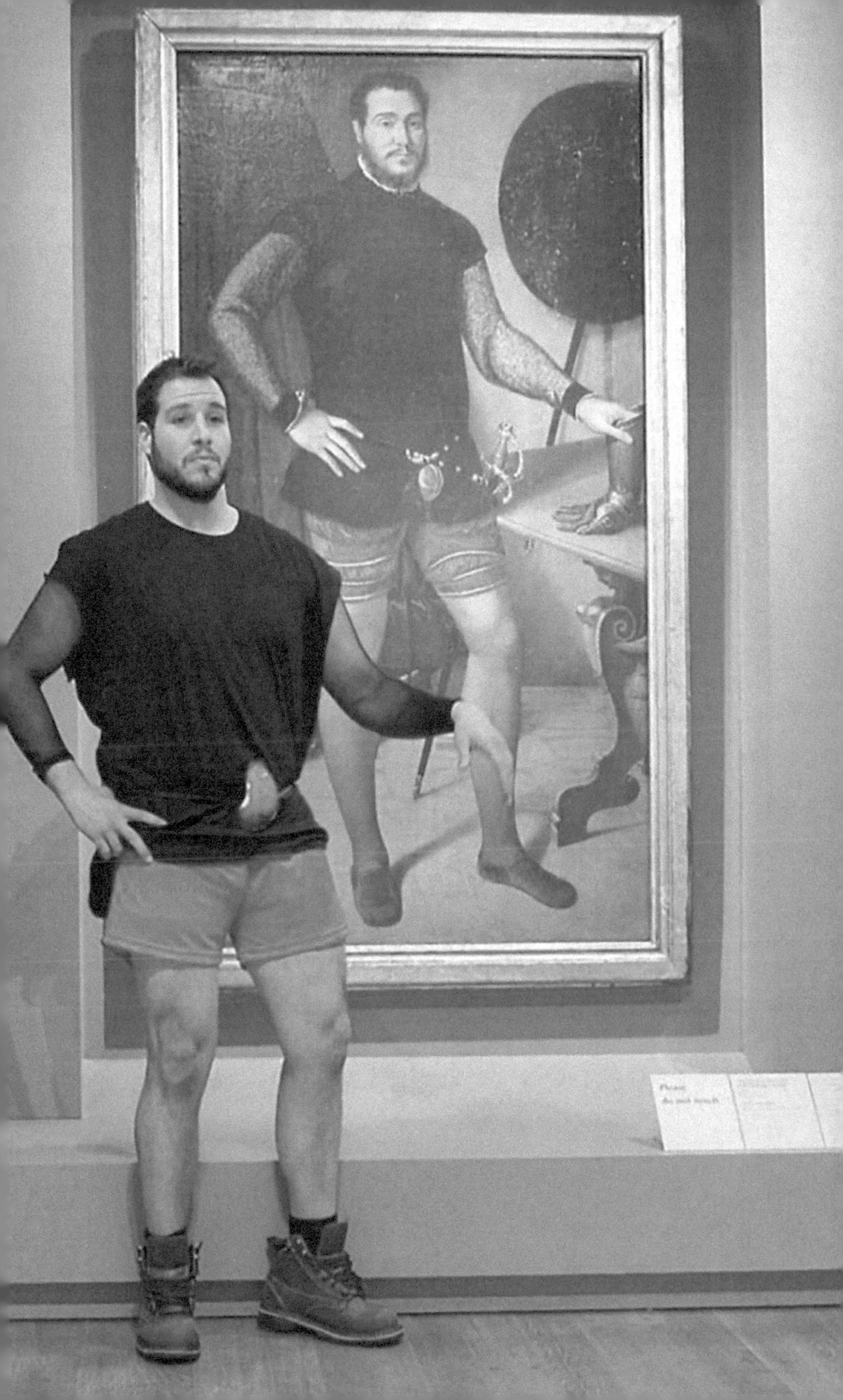

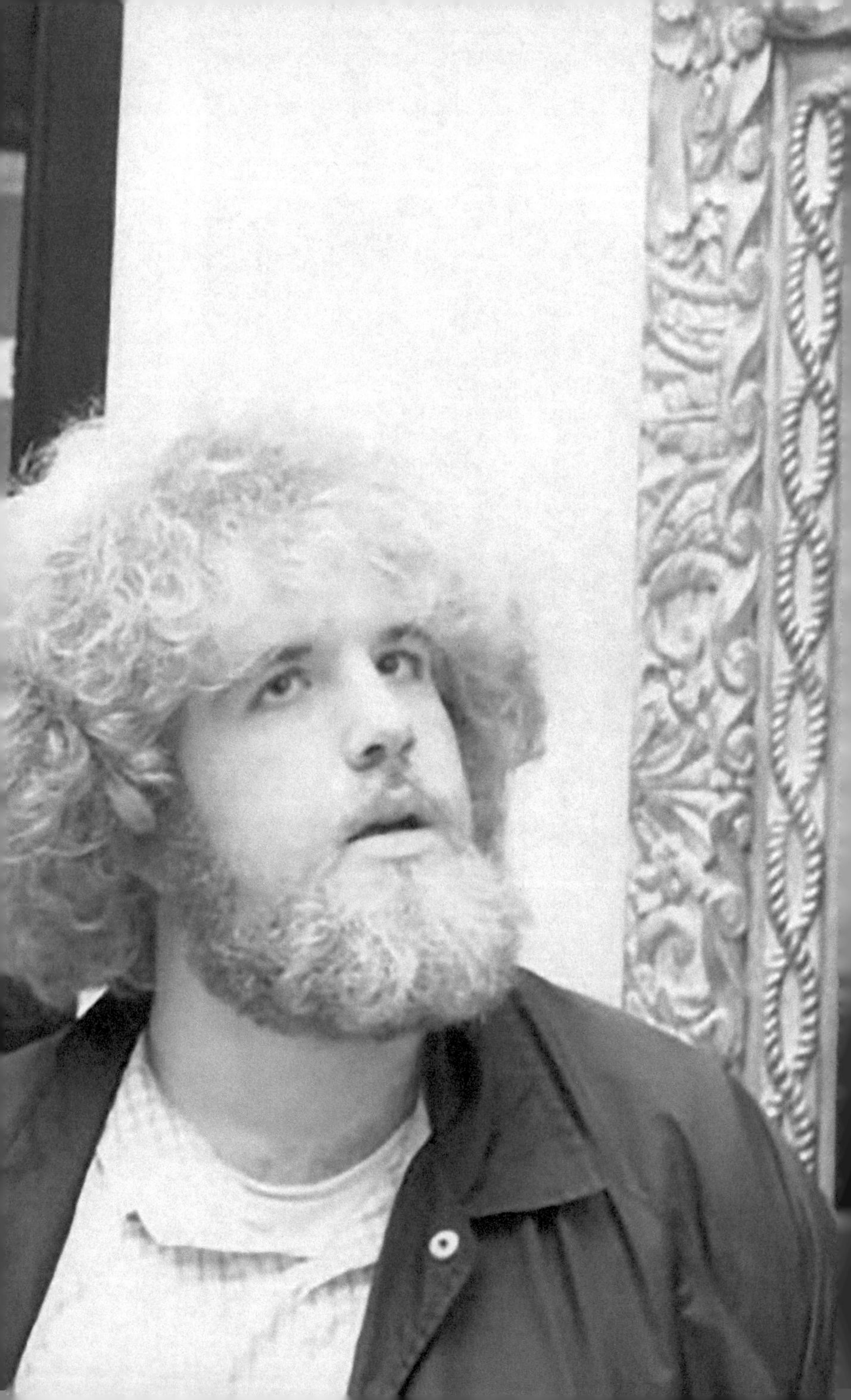

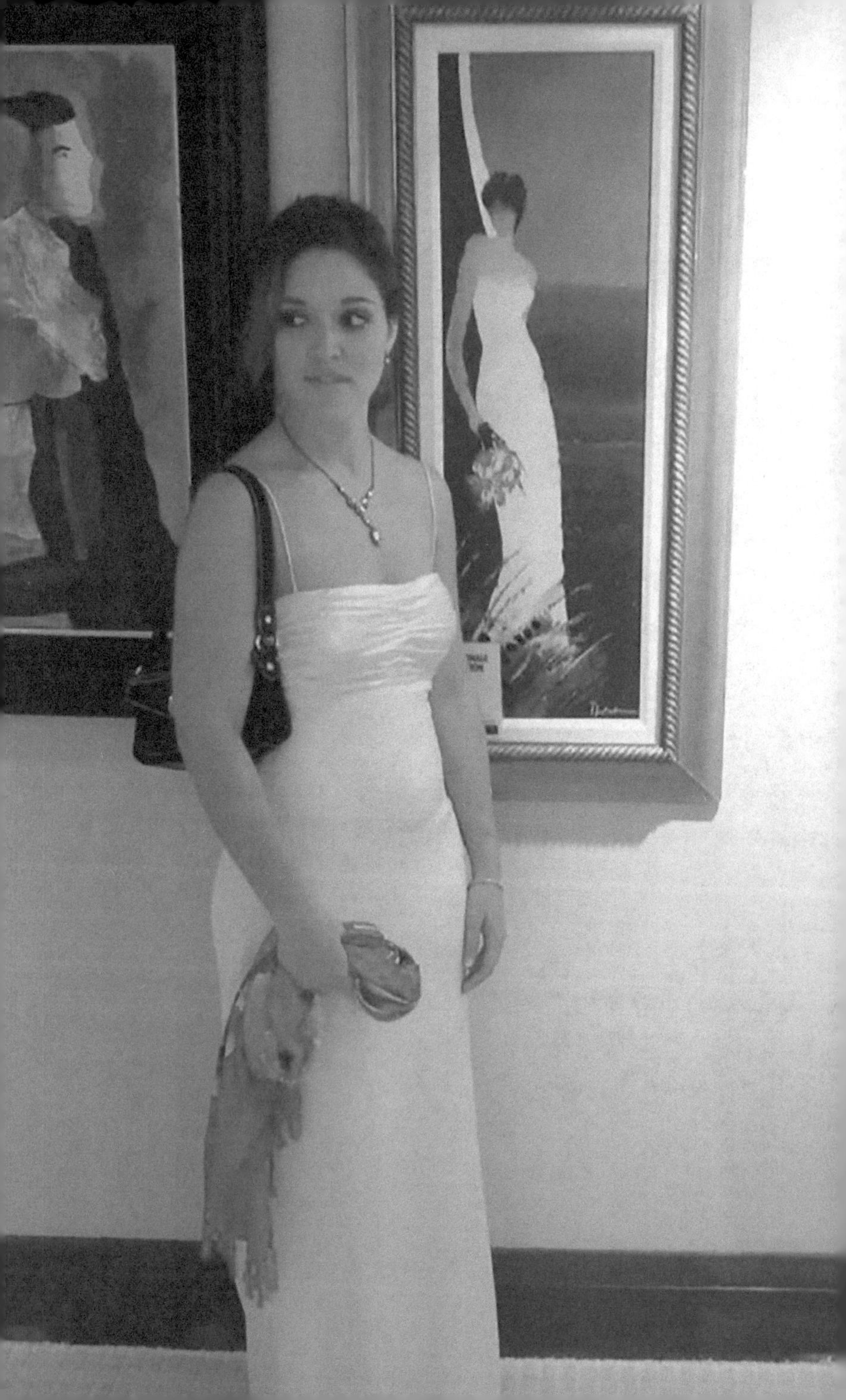

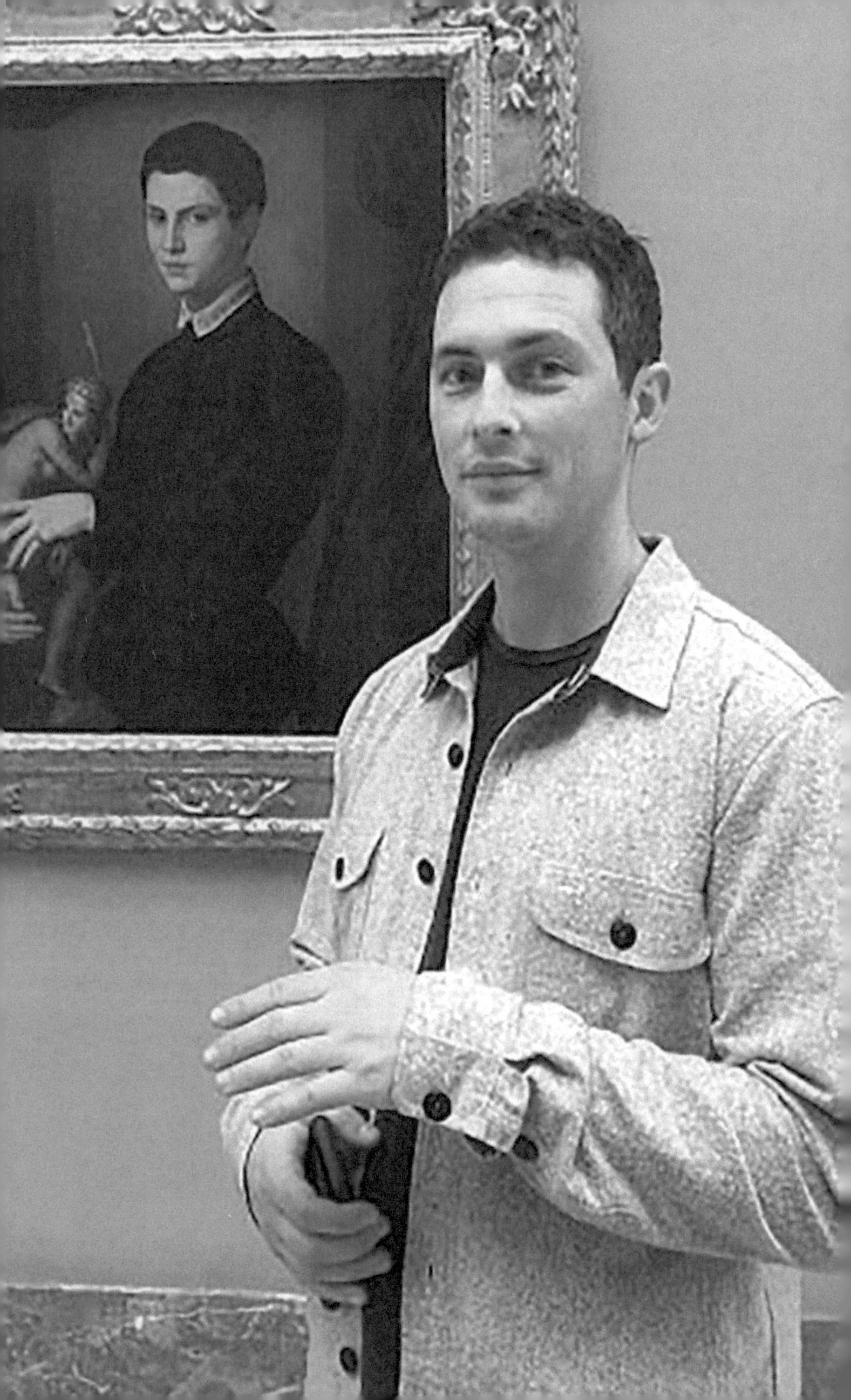

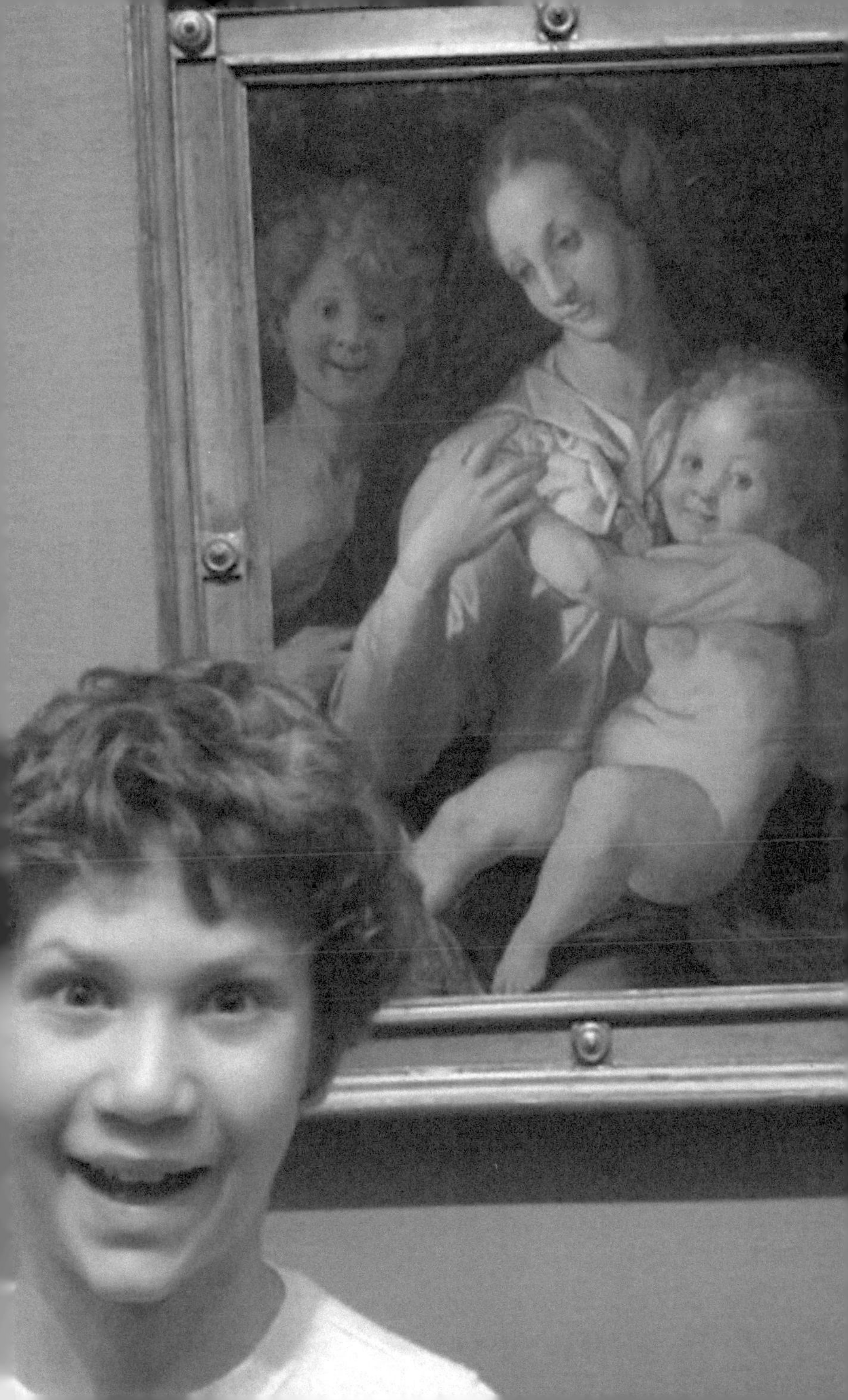

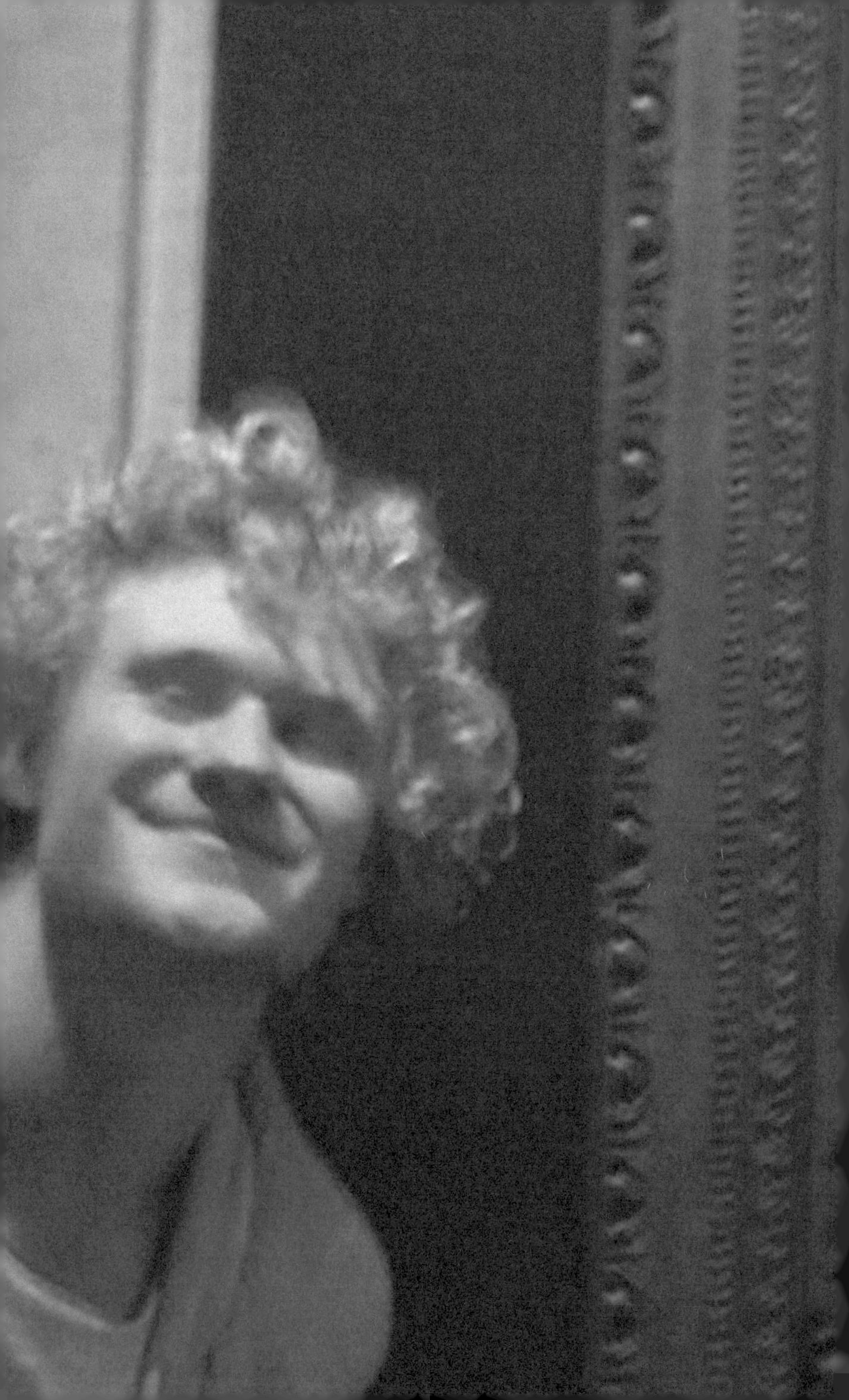

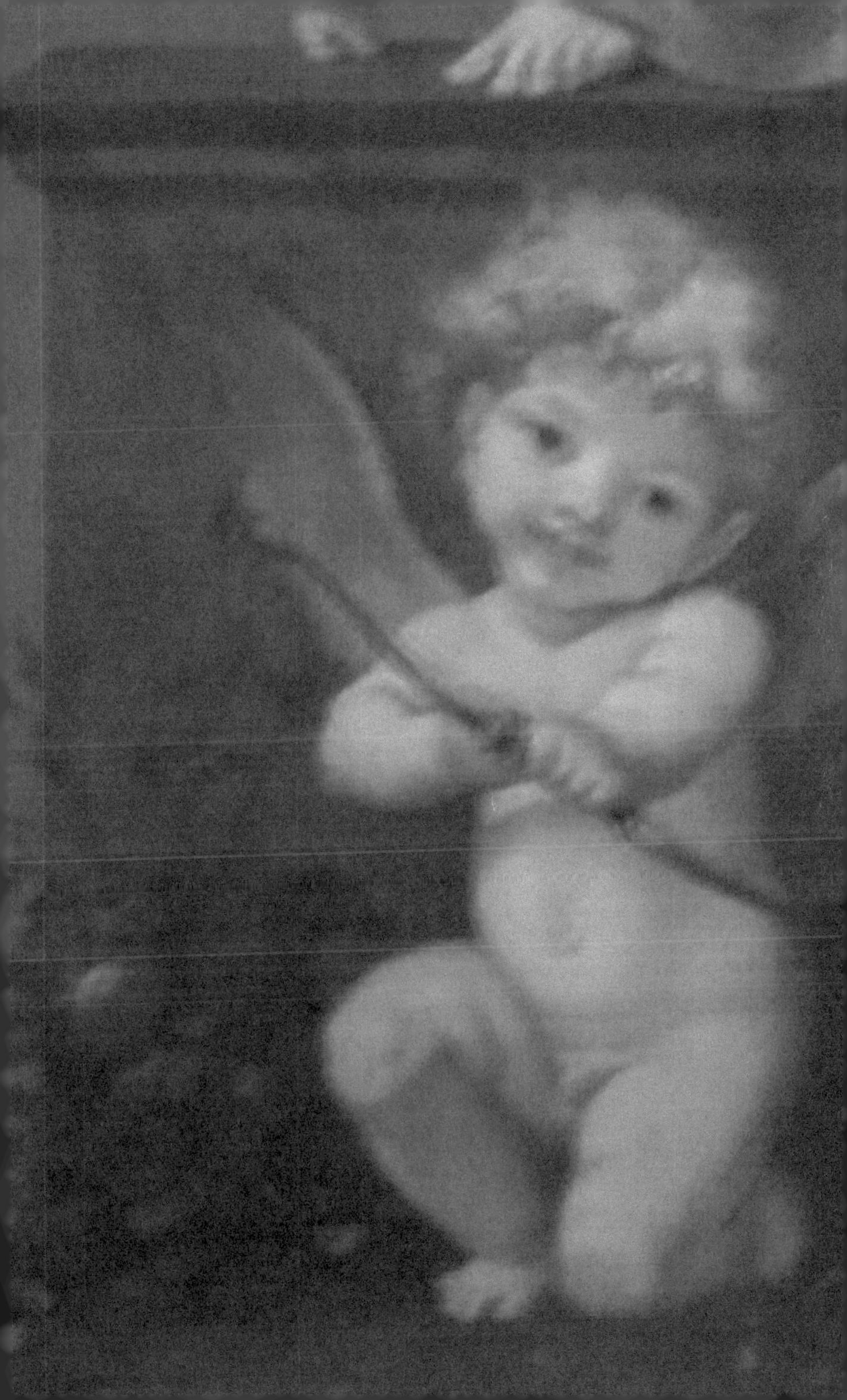

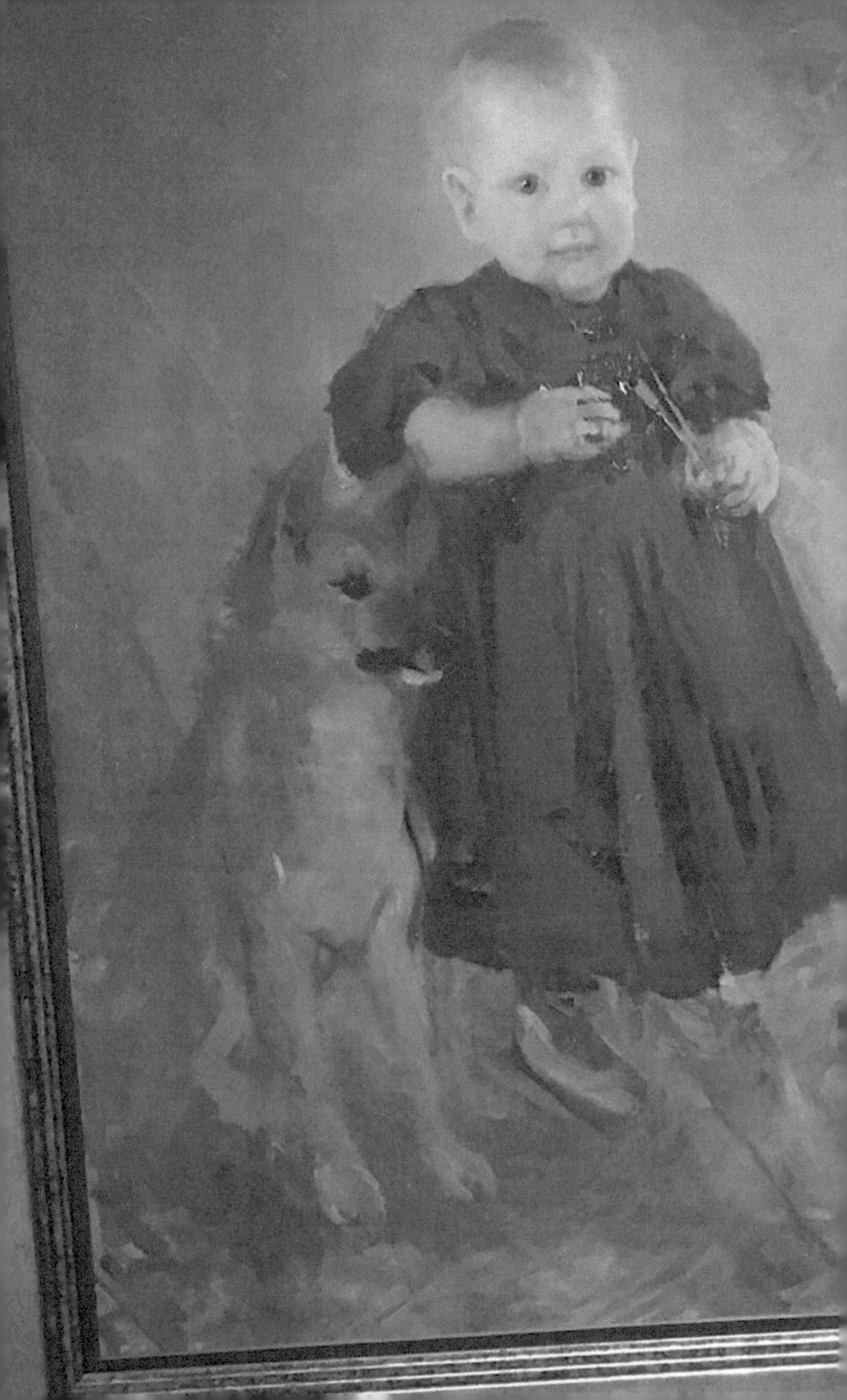

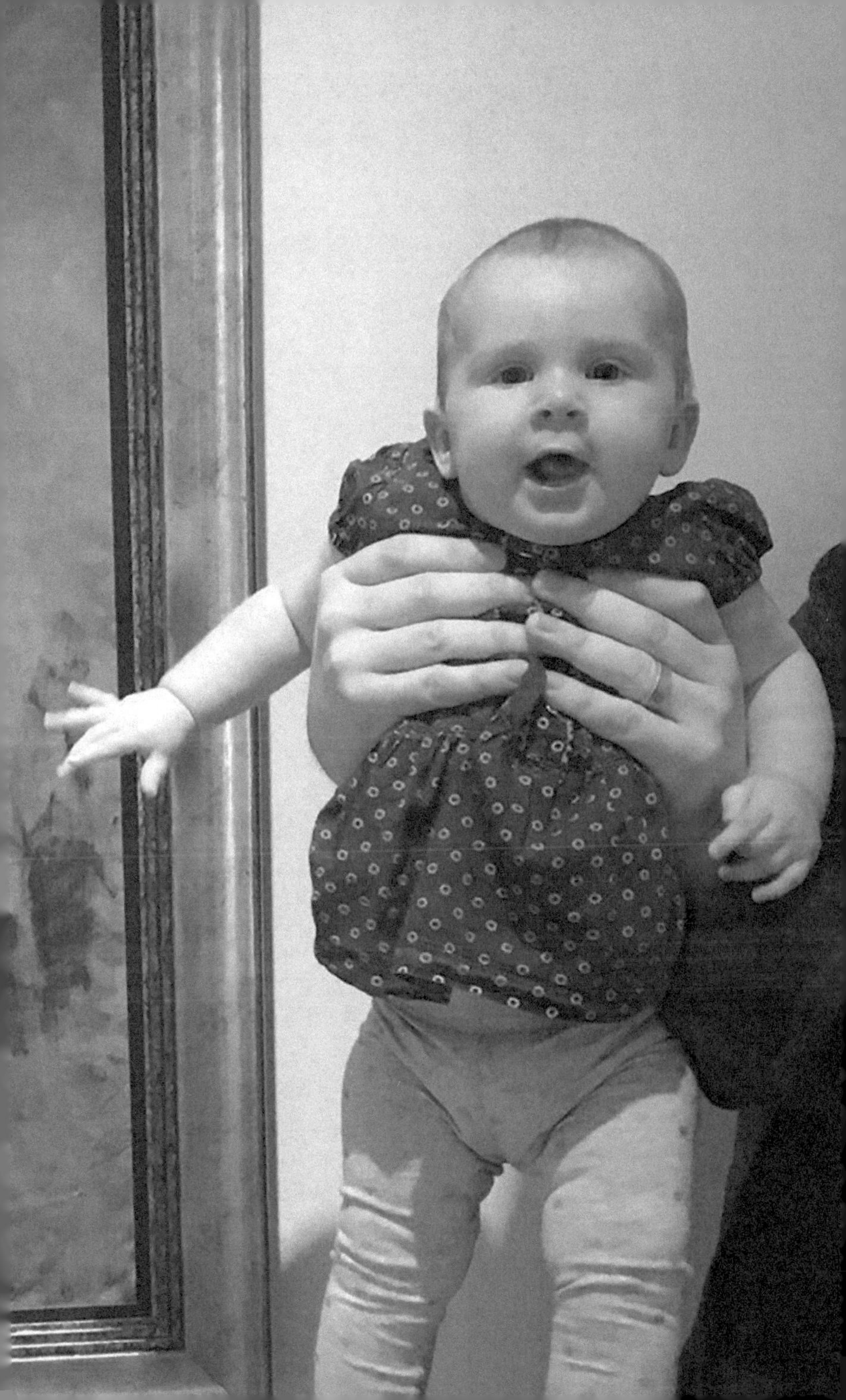

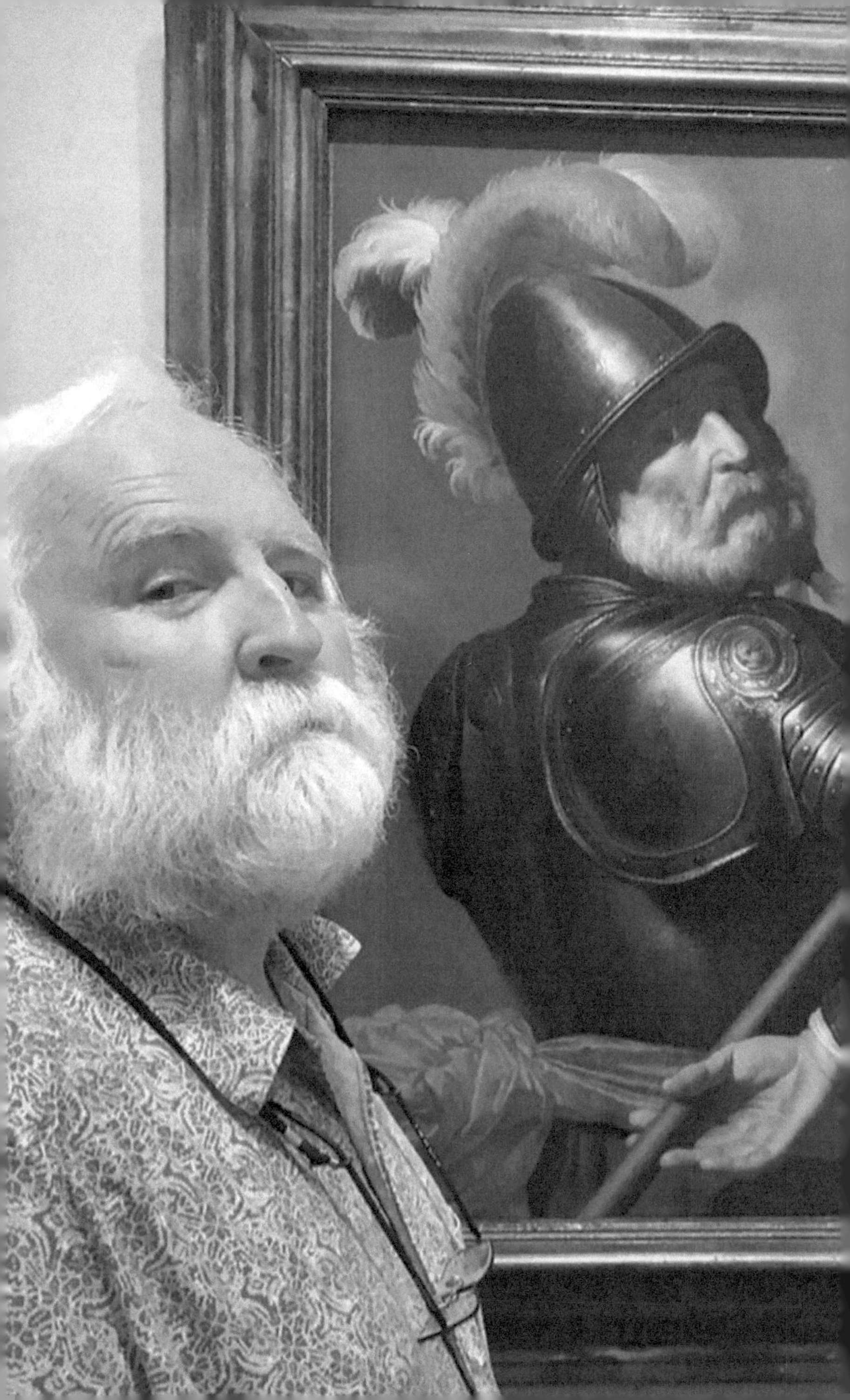

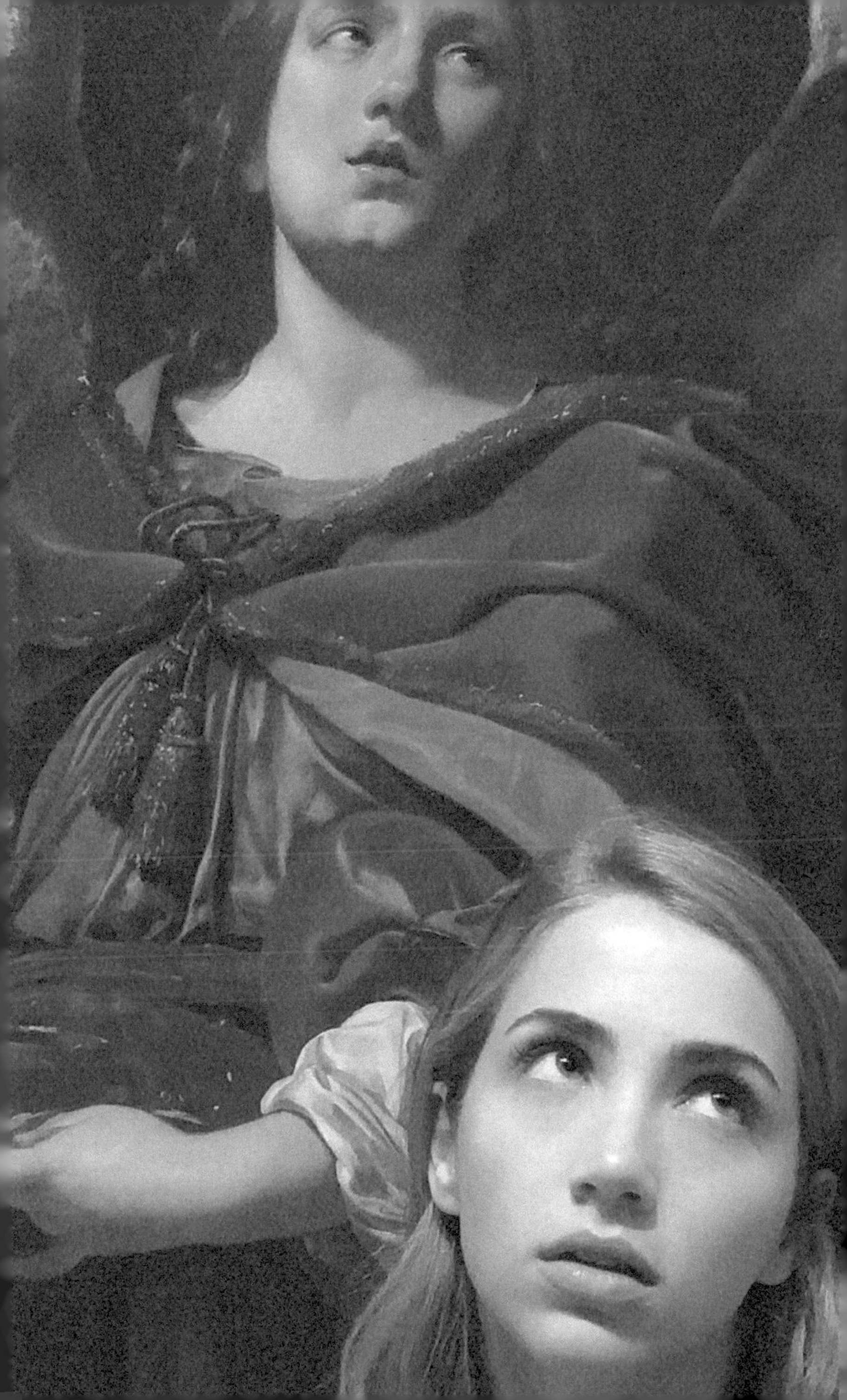

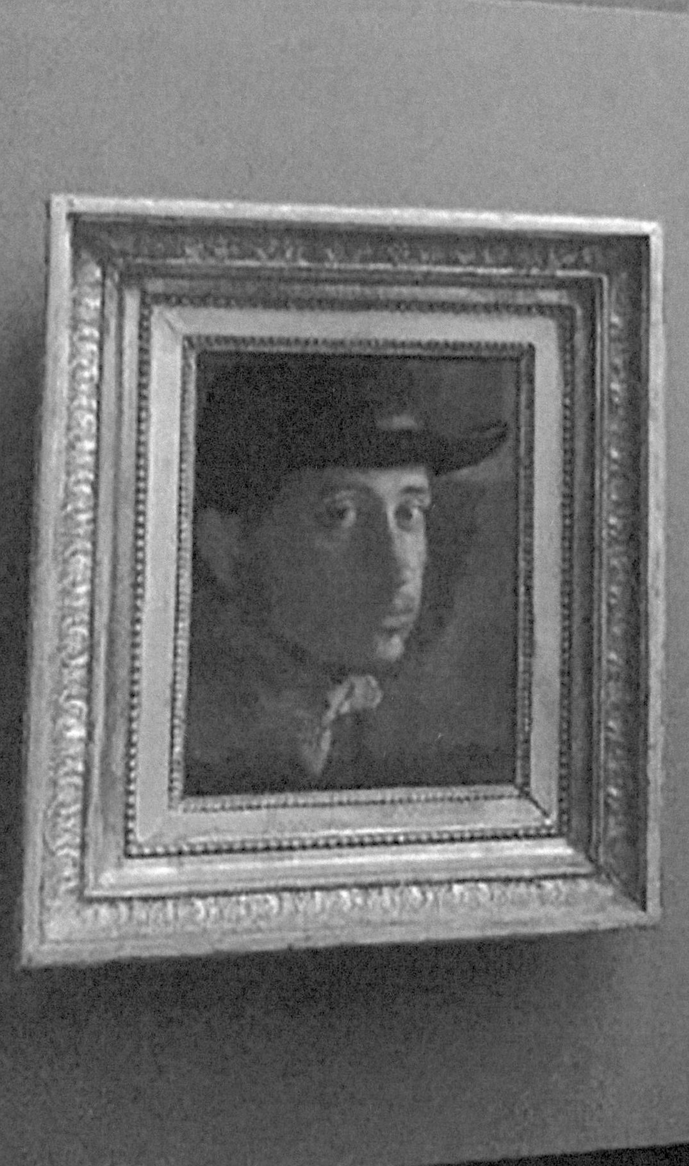

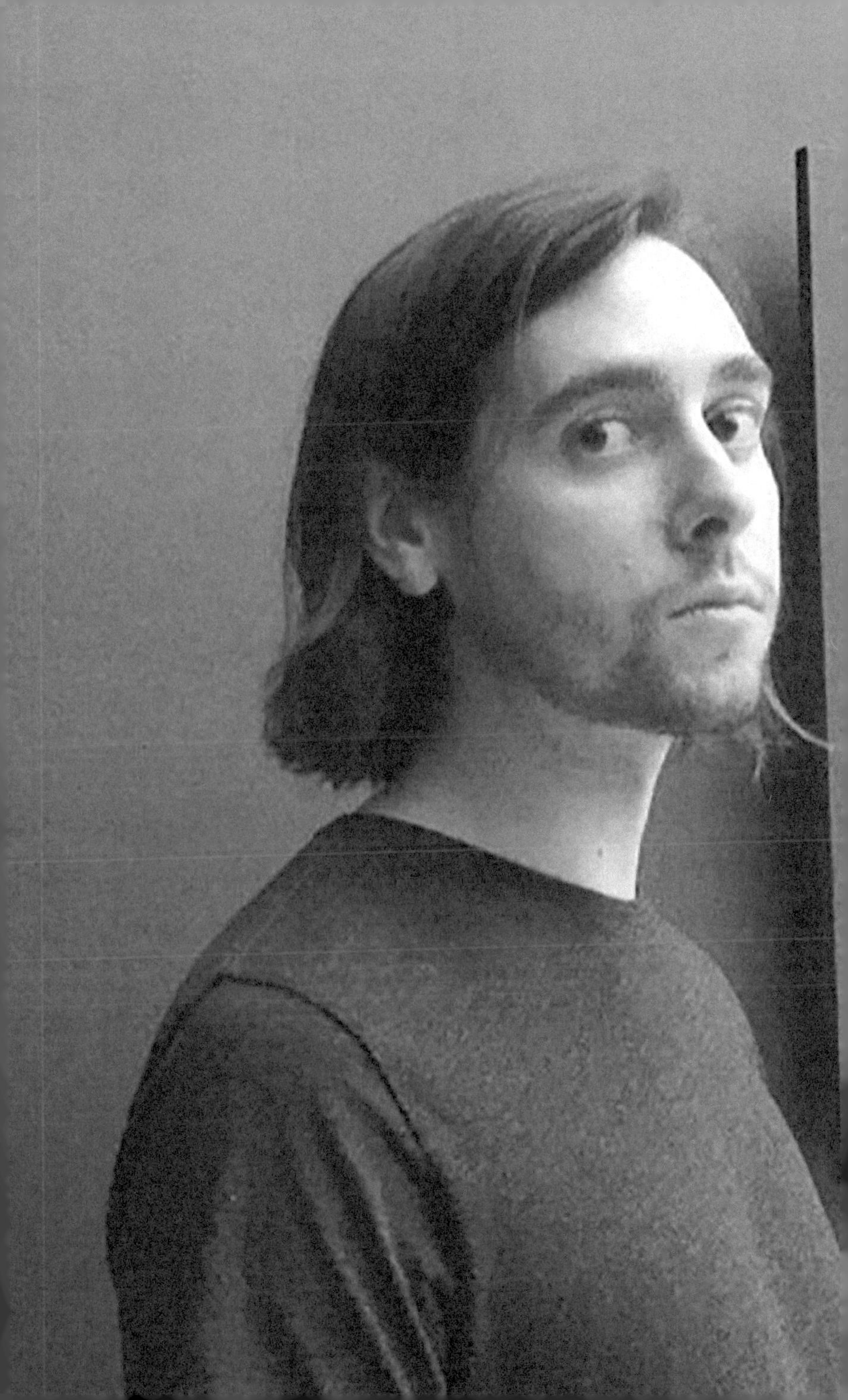

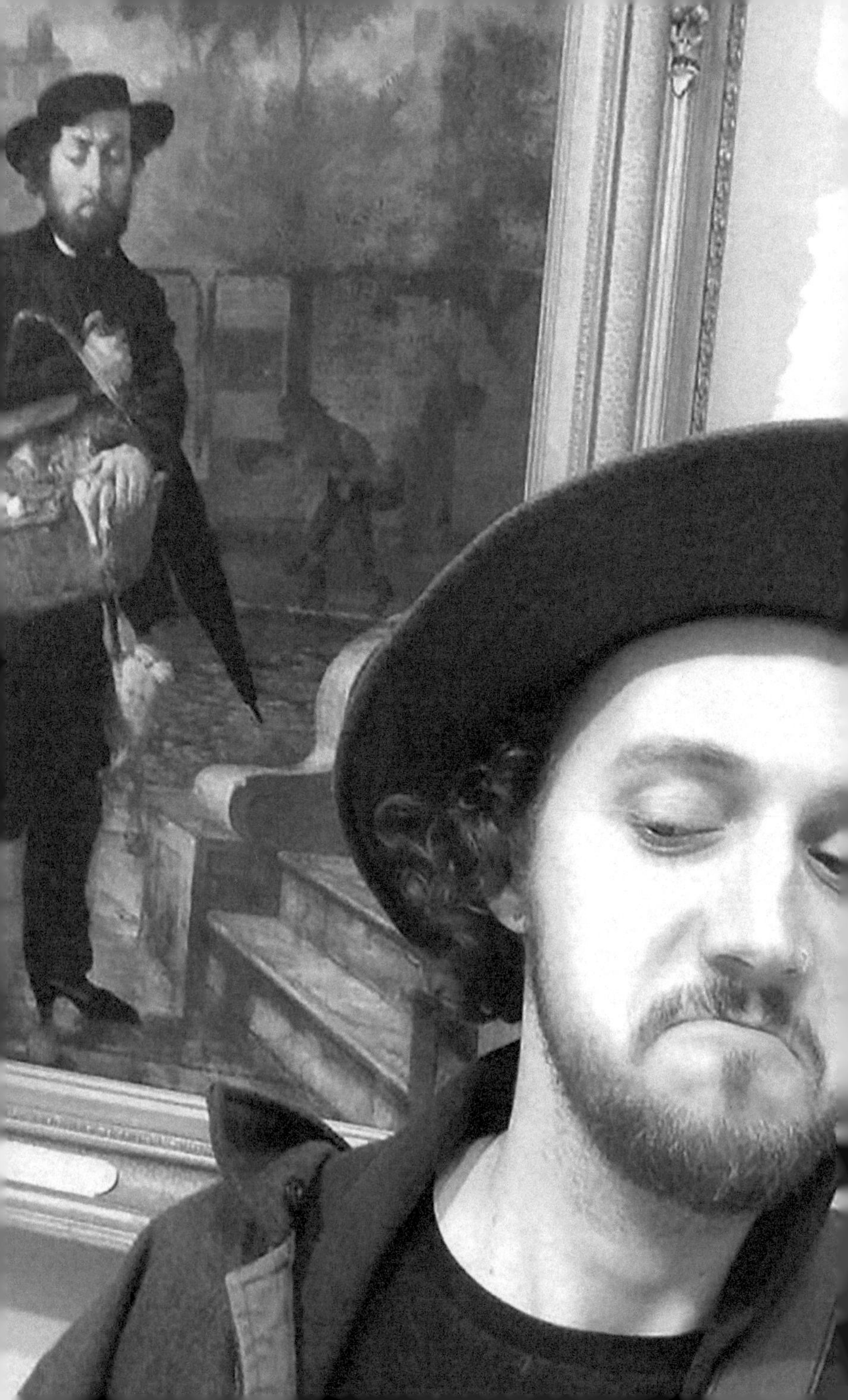

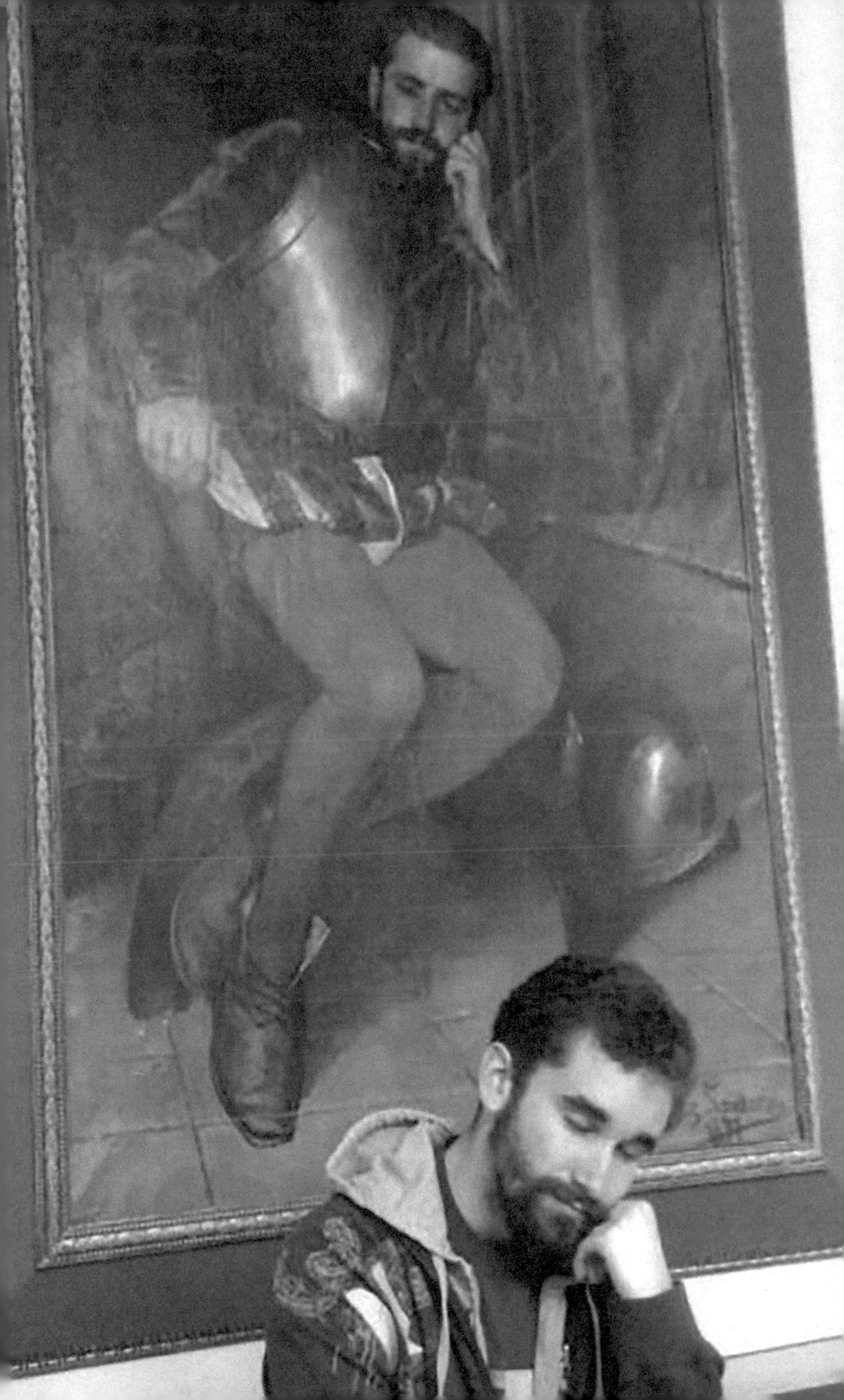

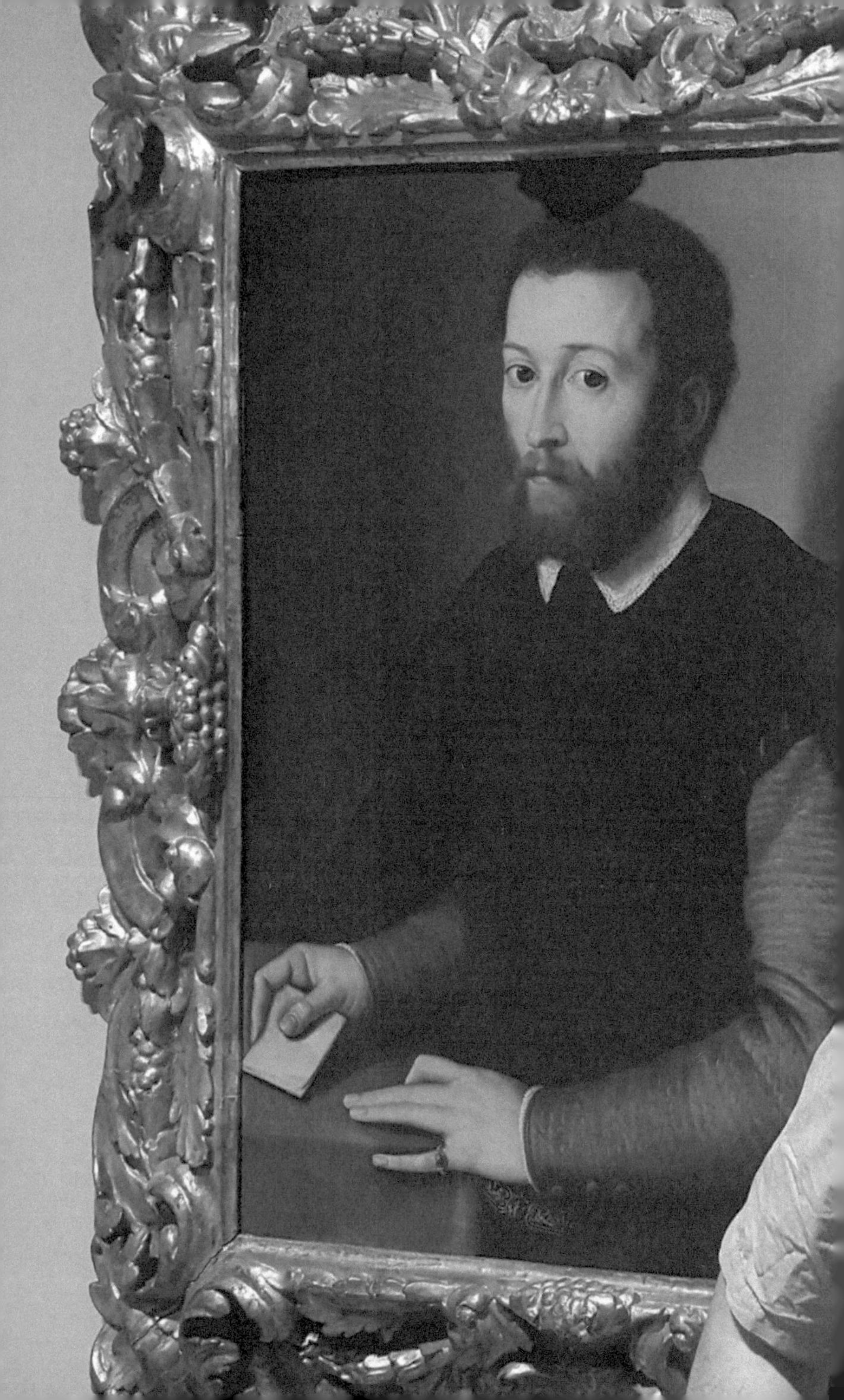

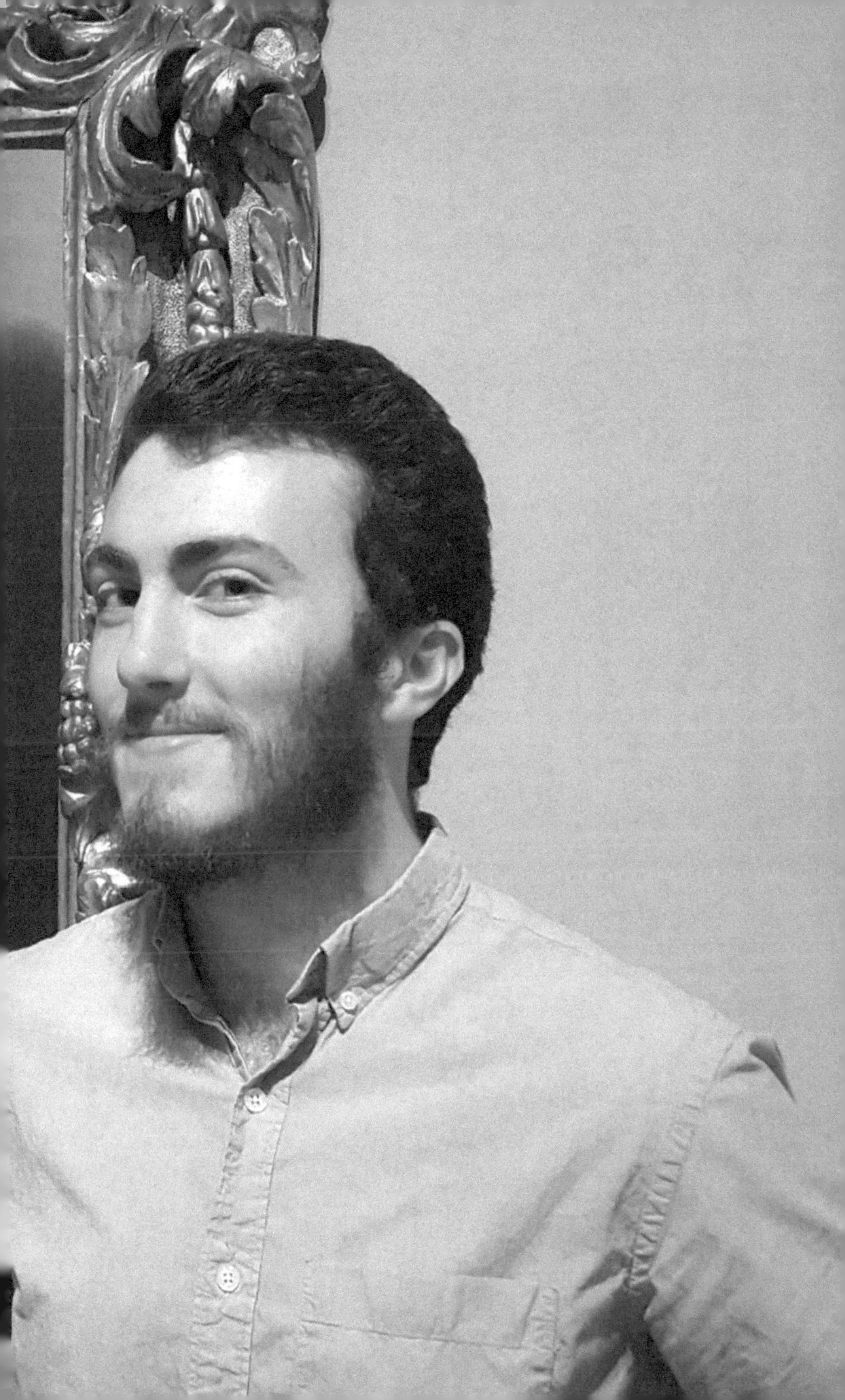

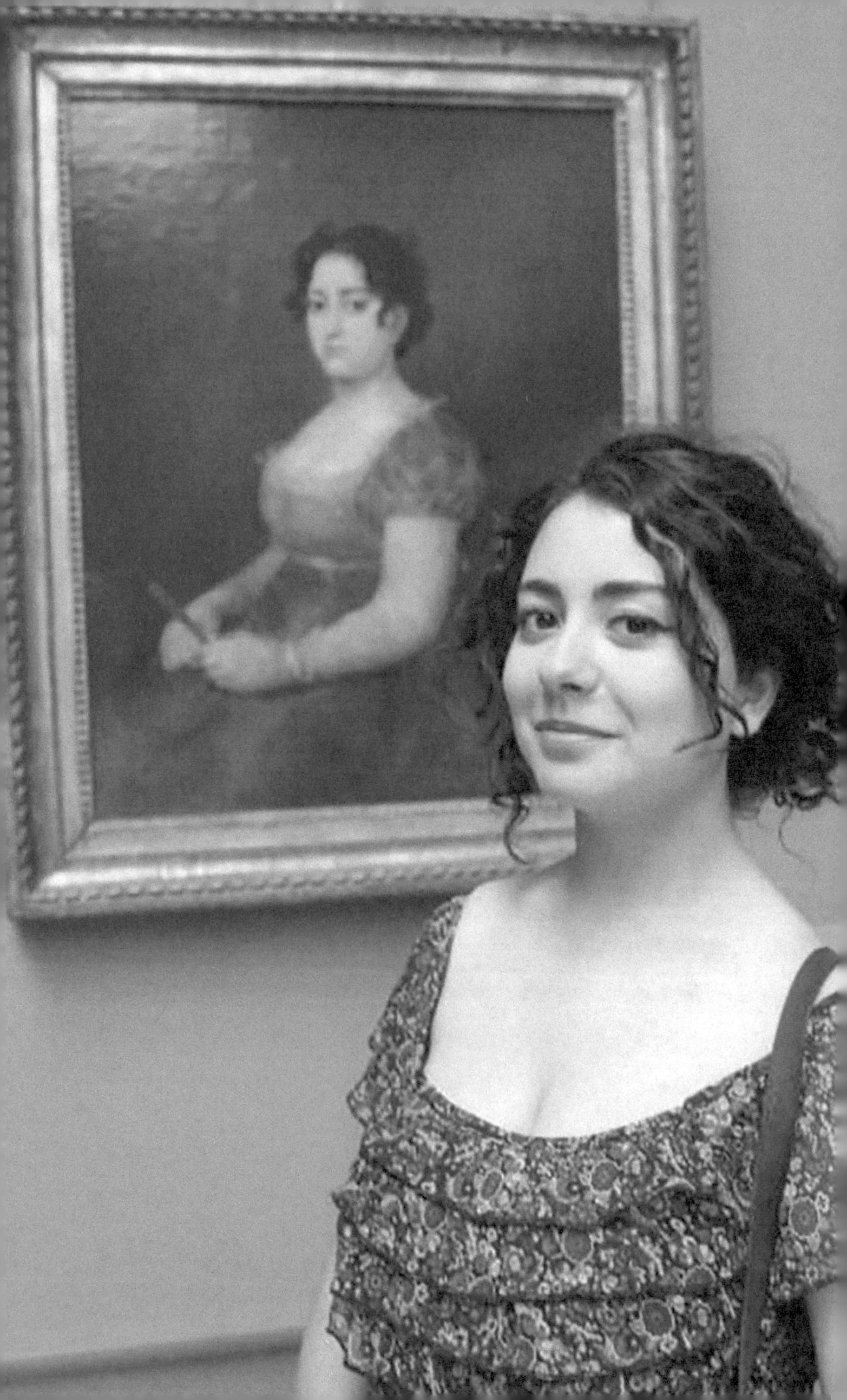

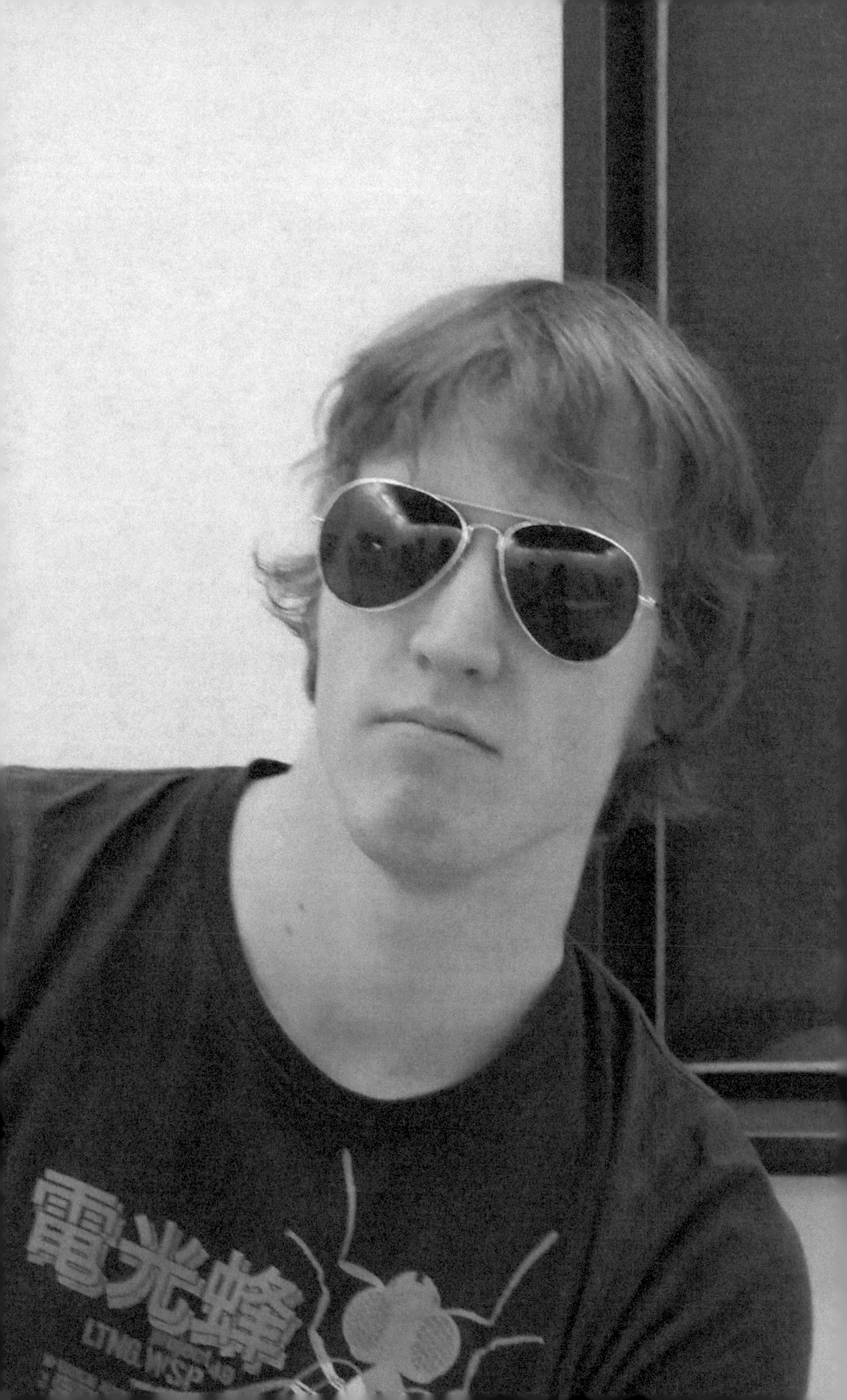
電光蜂

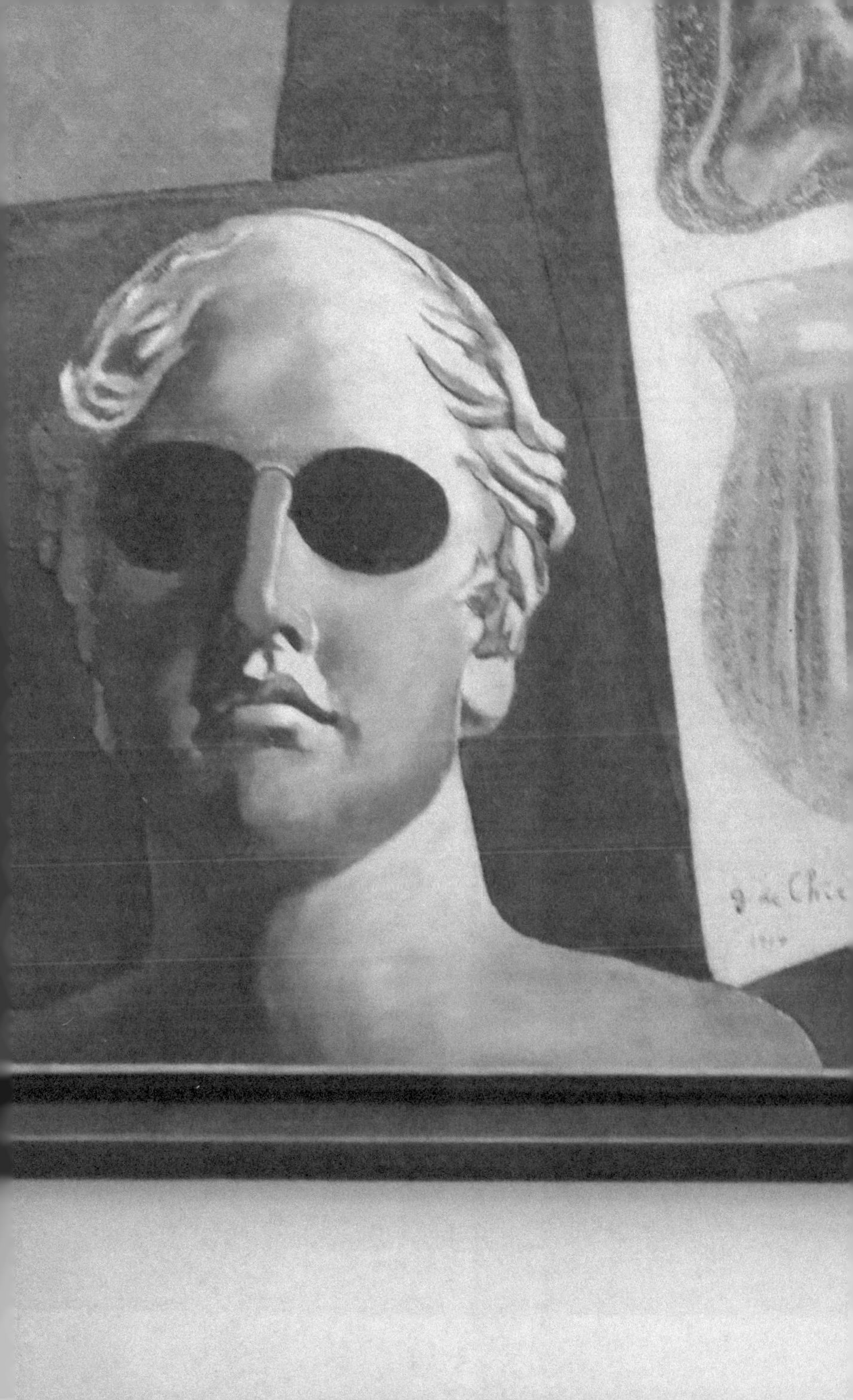

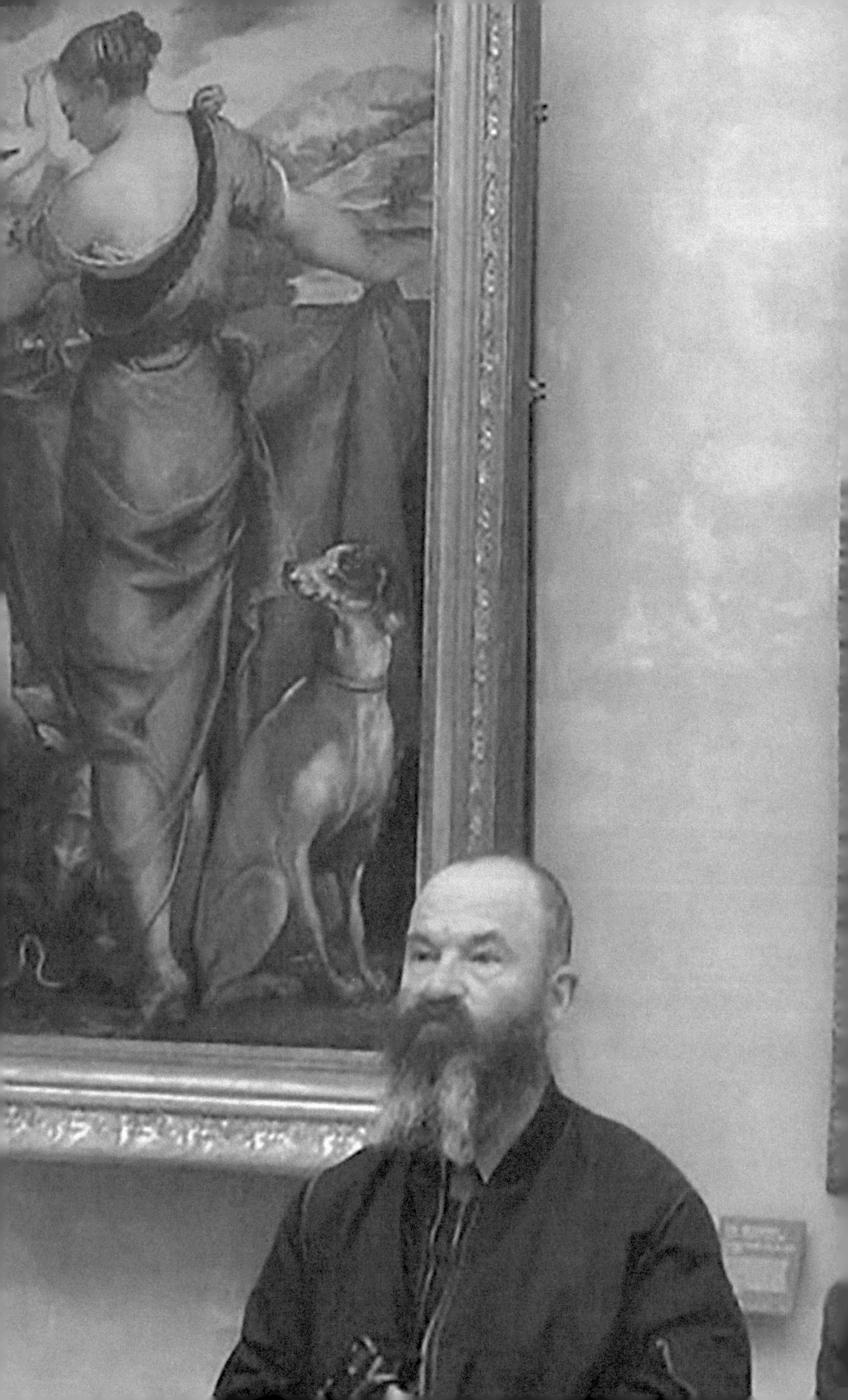

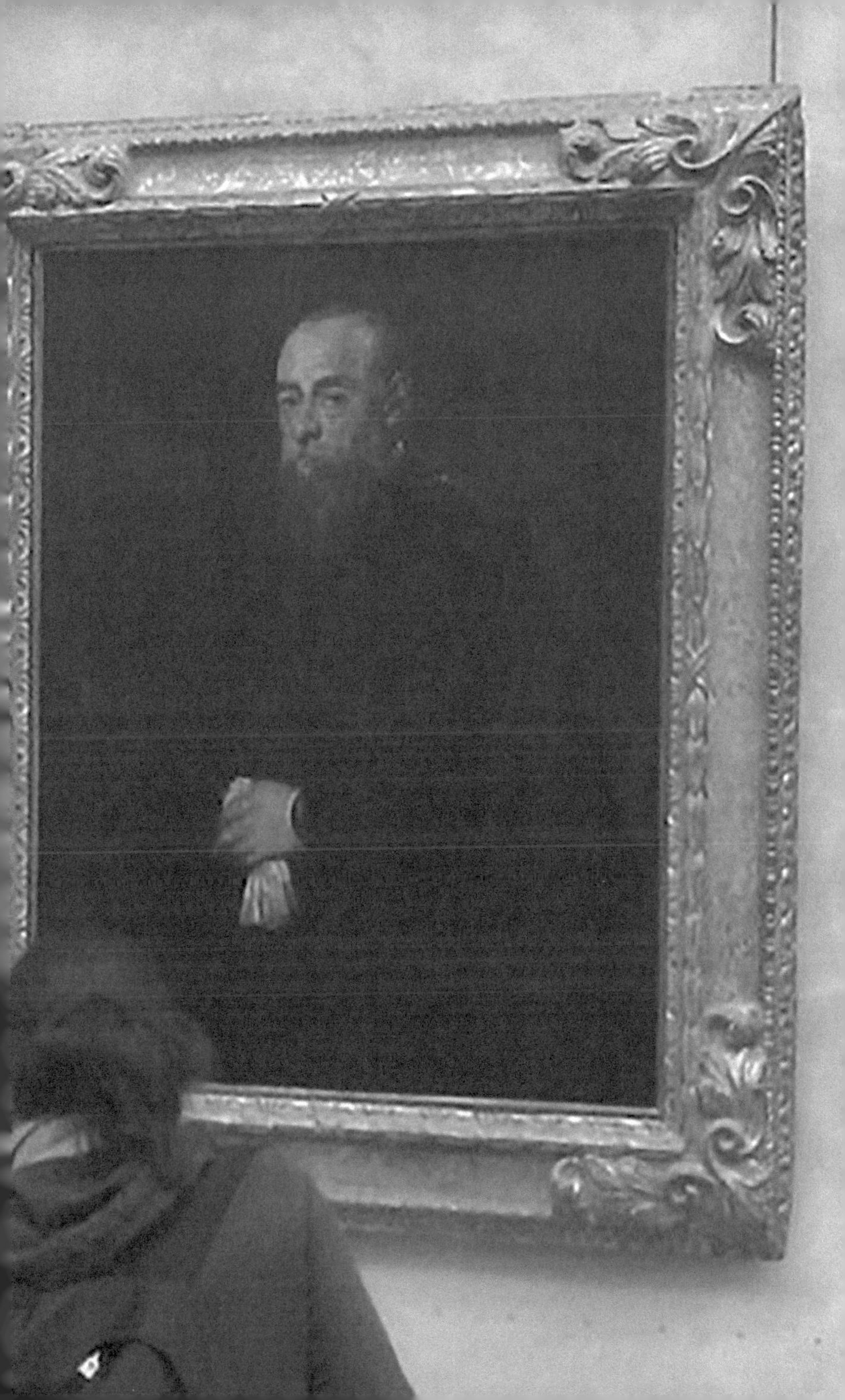

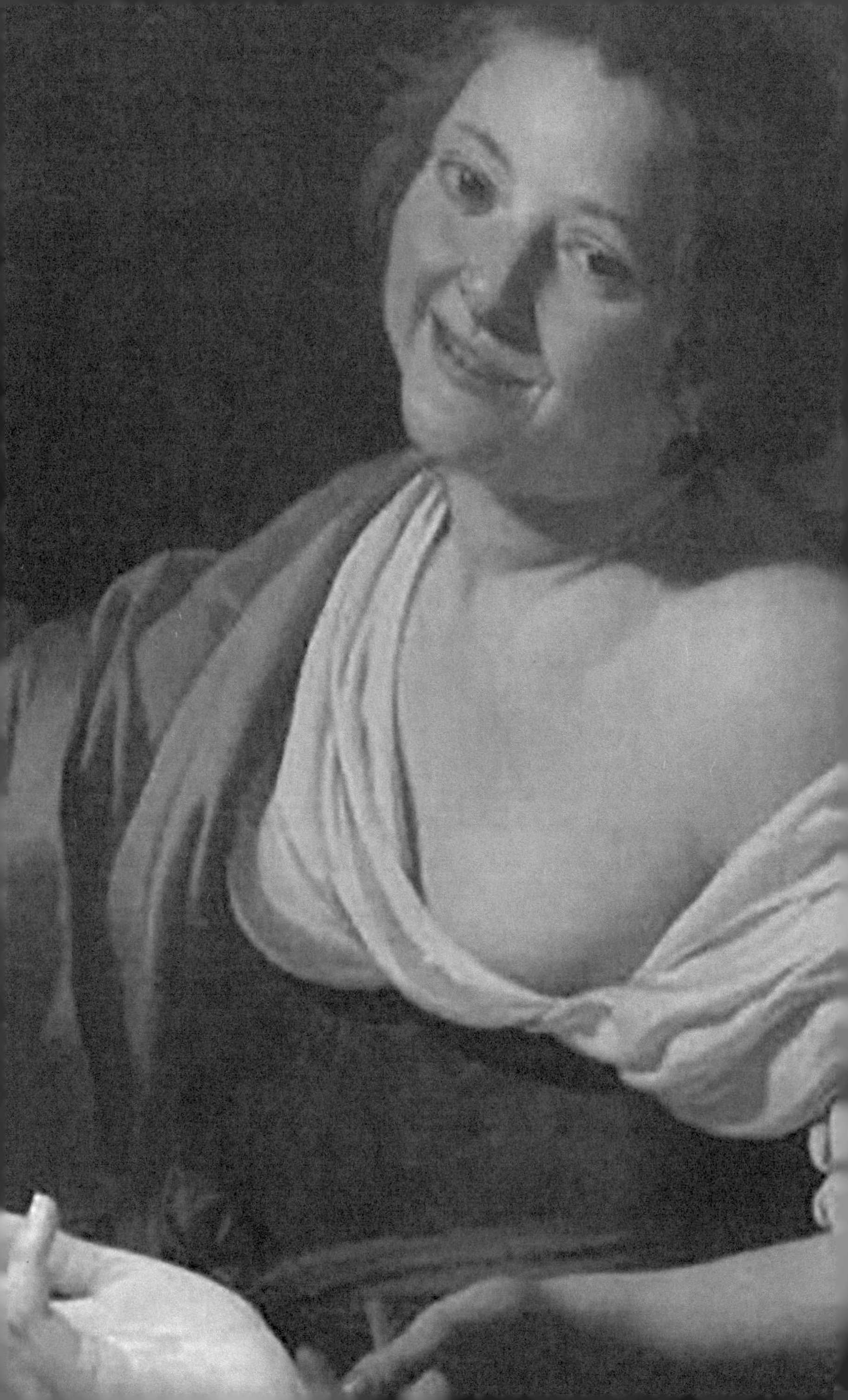

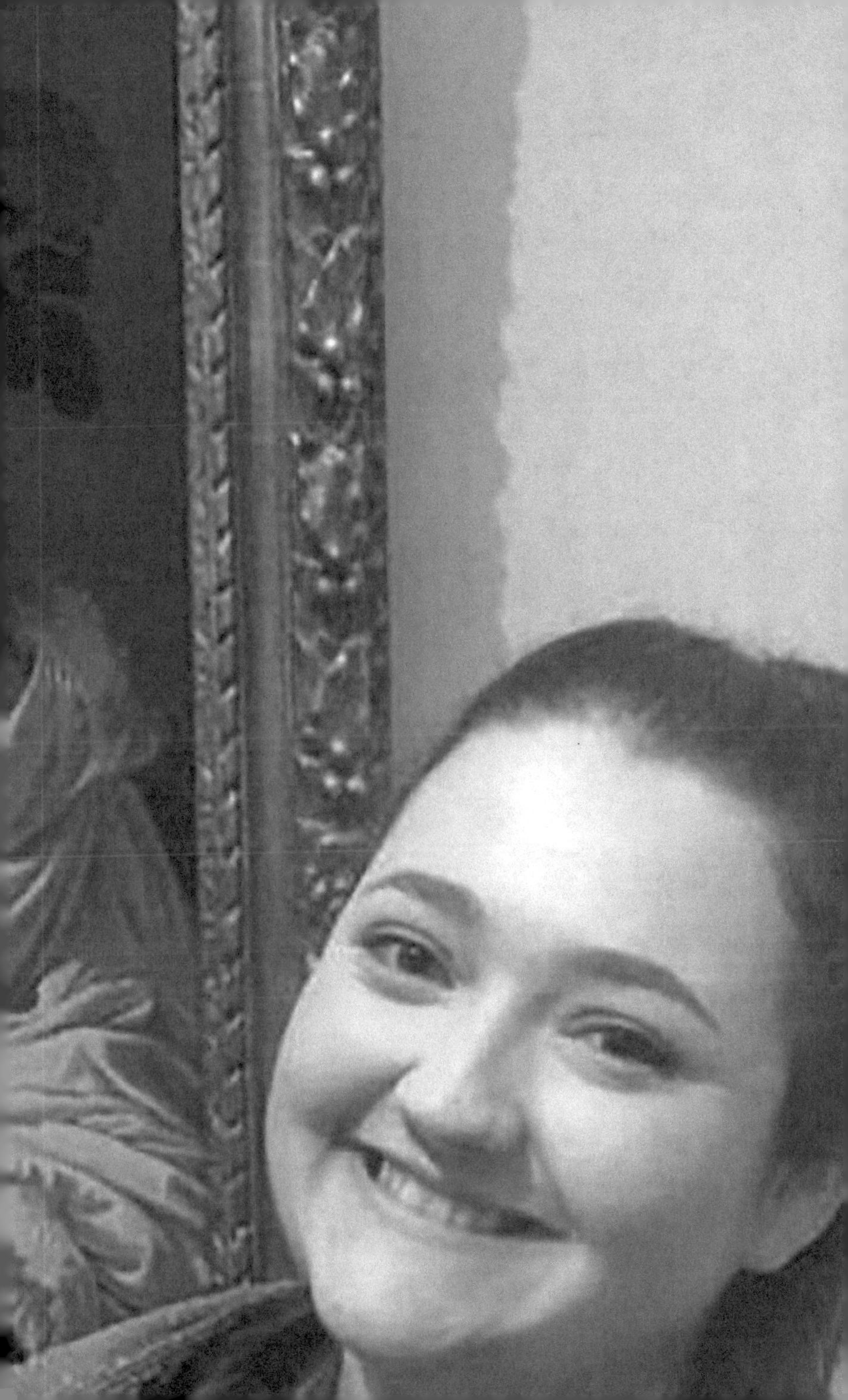

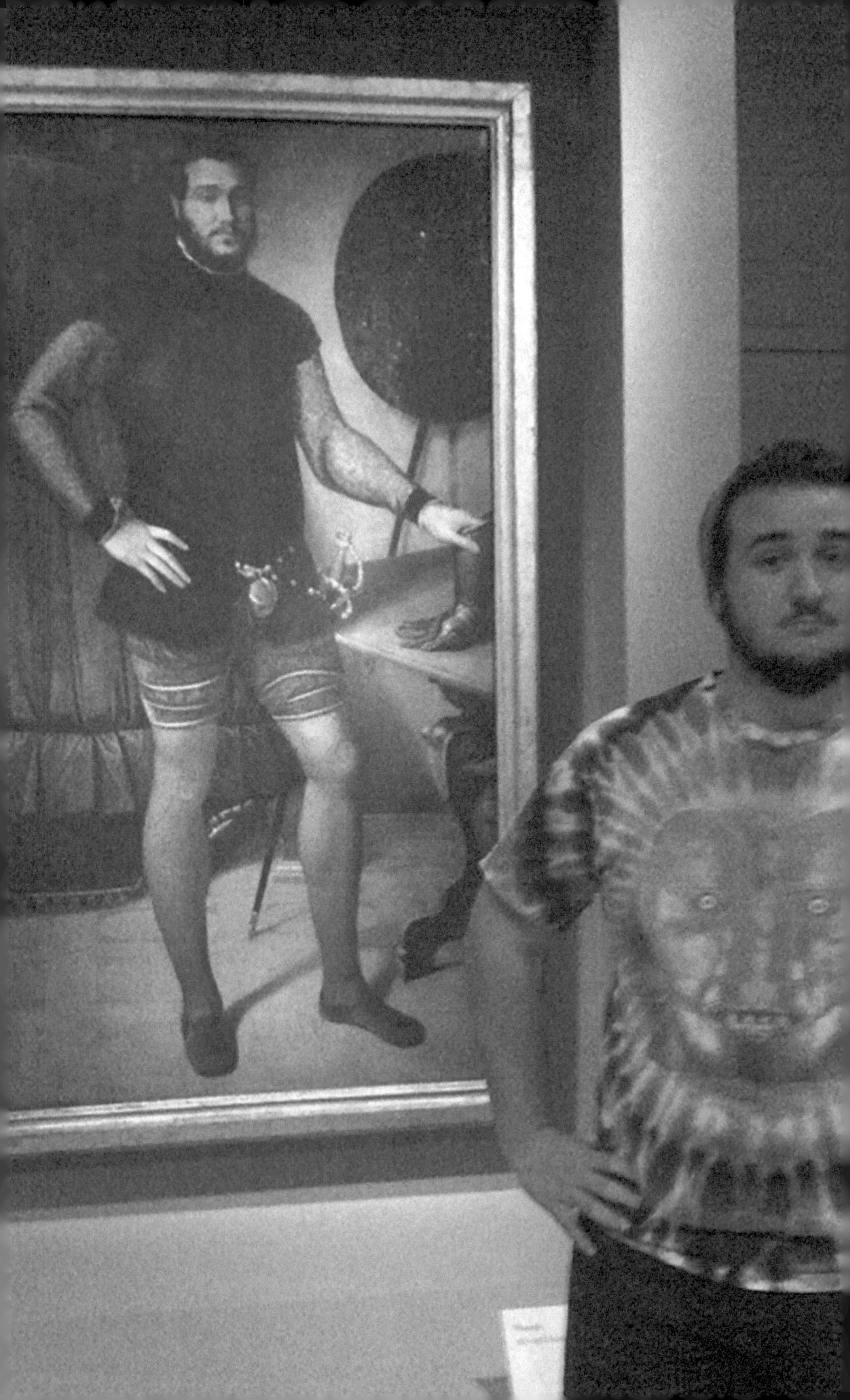

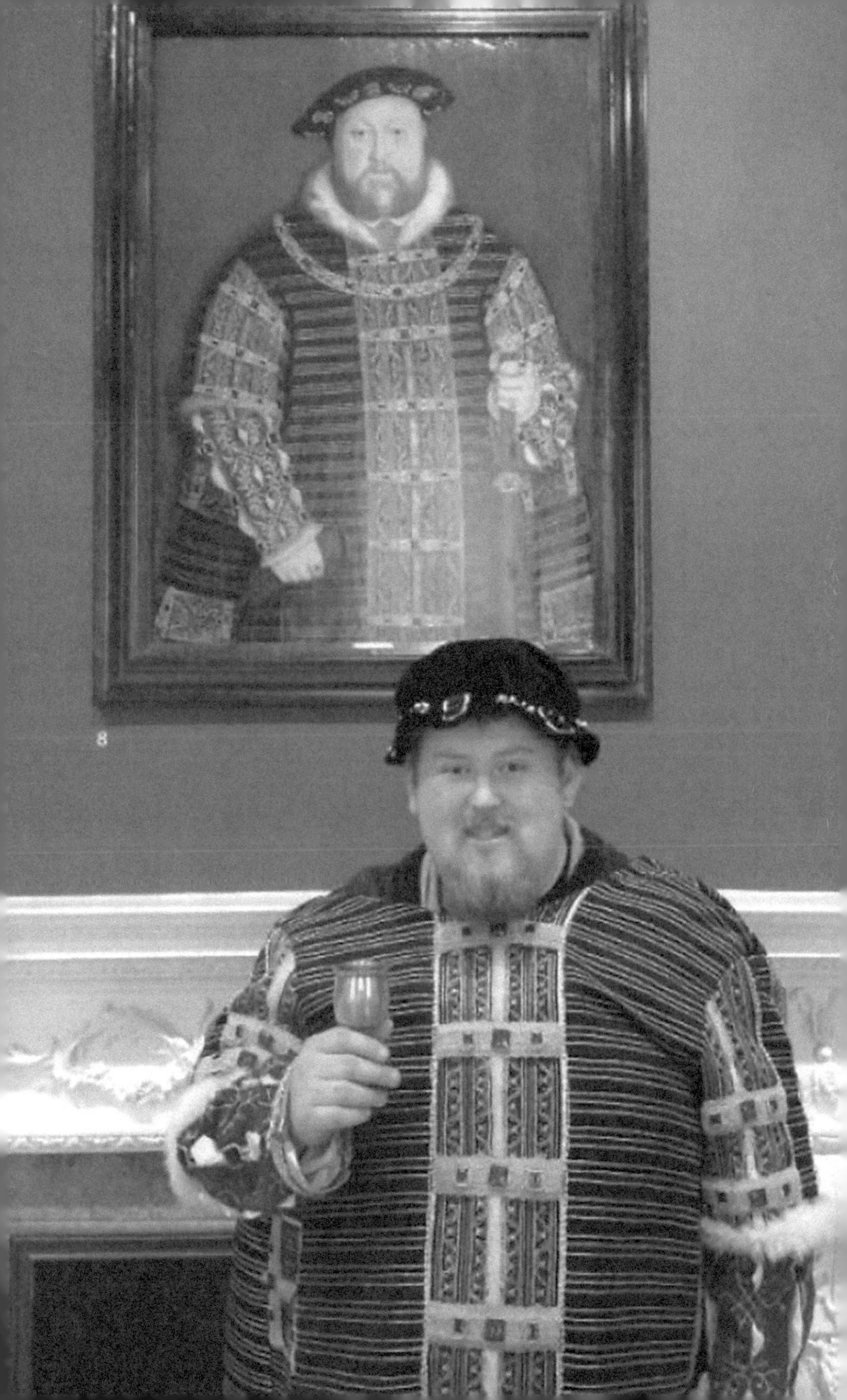
8

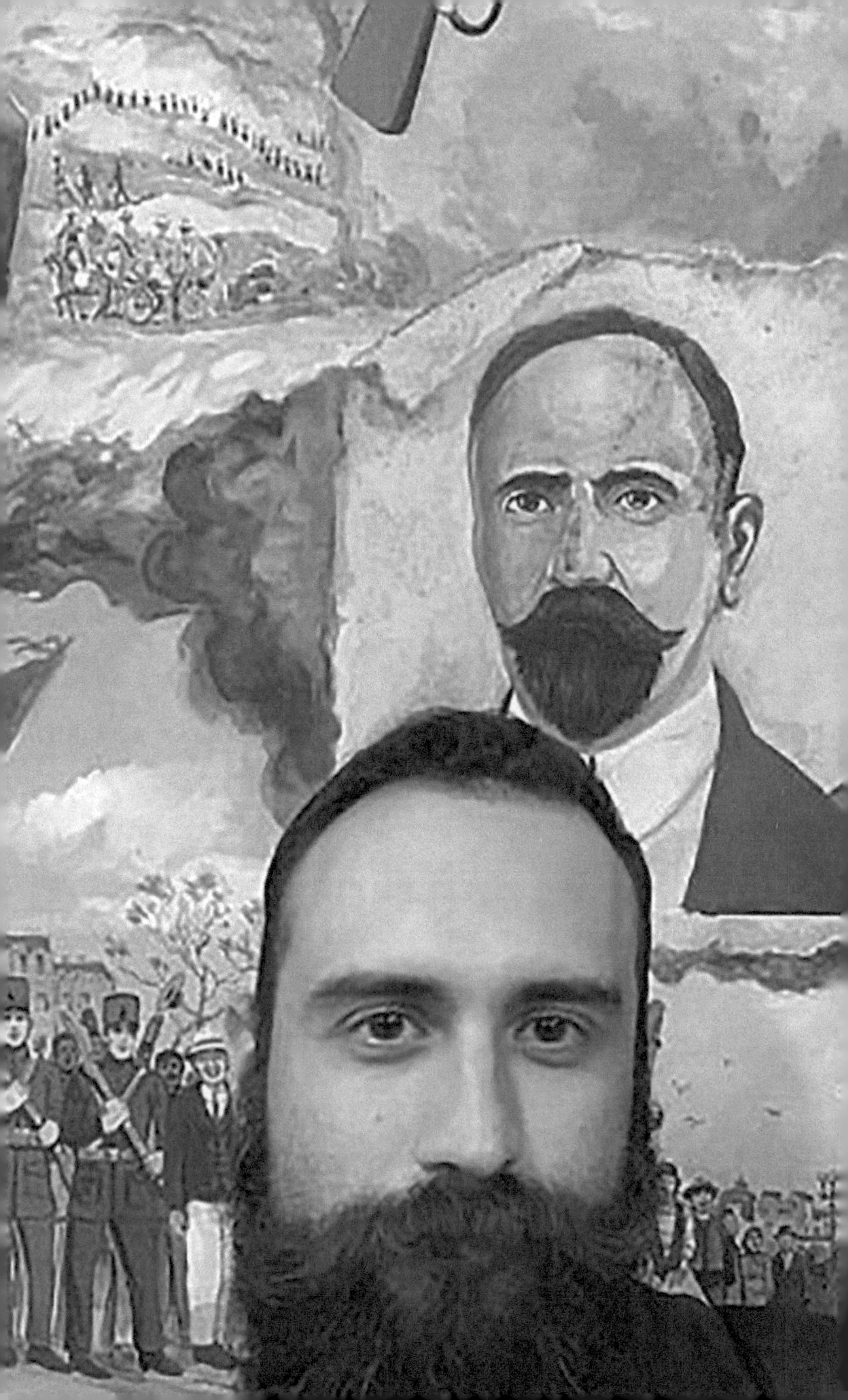

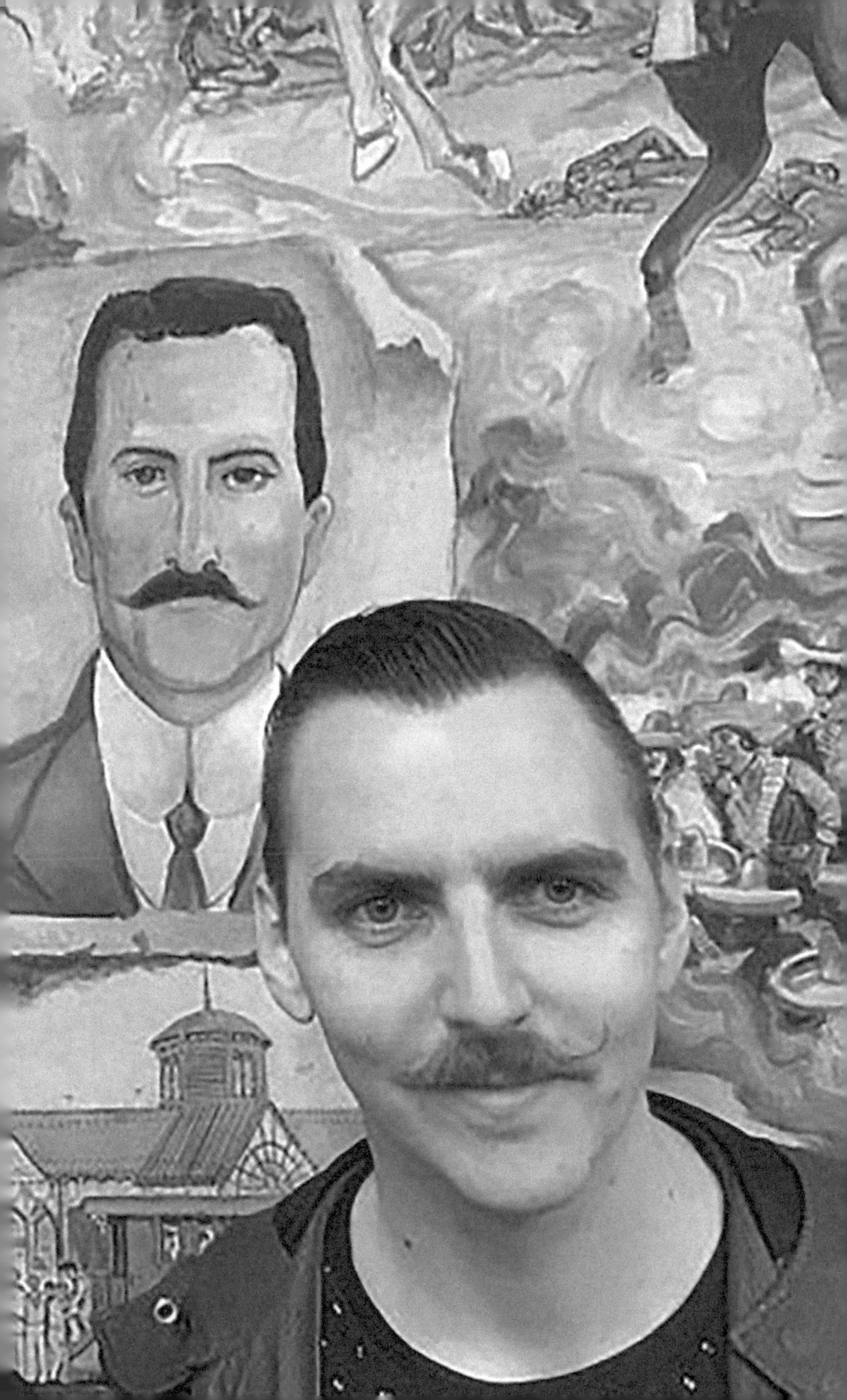

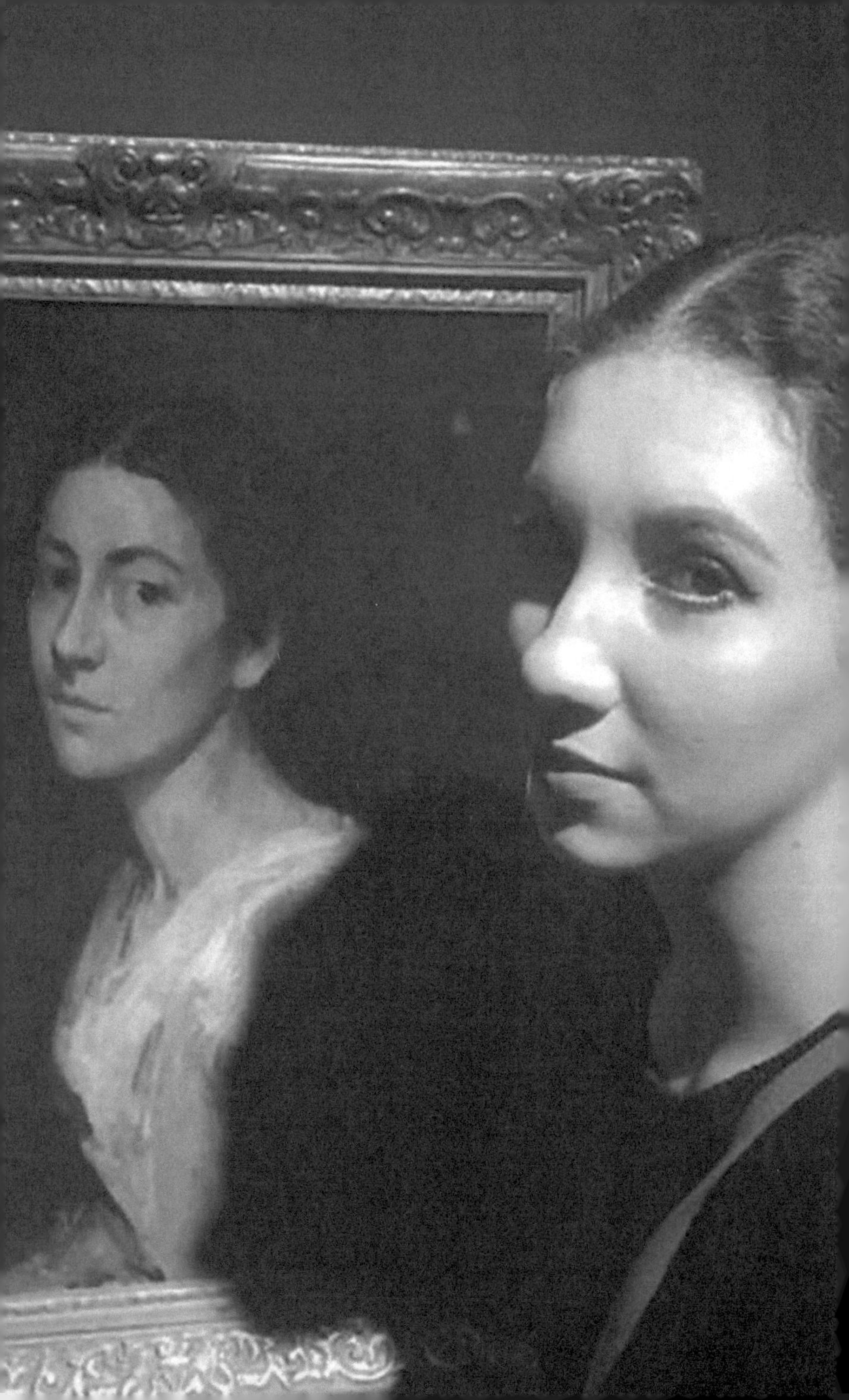

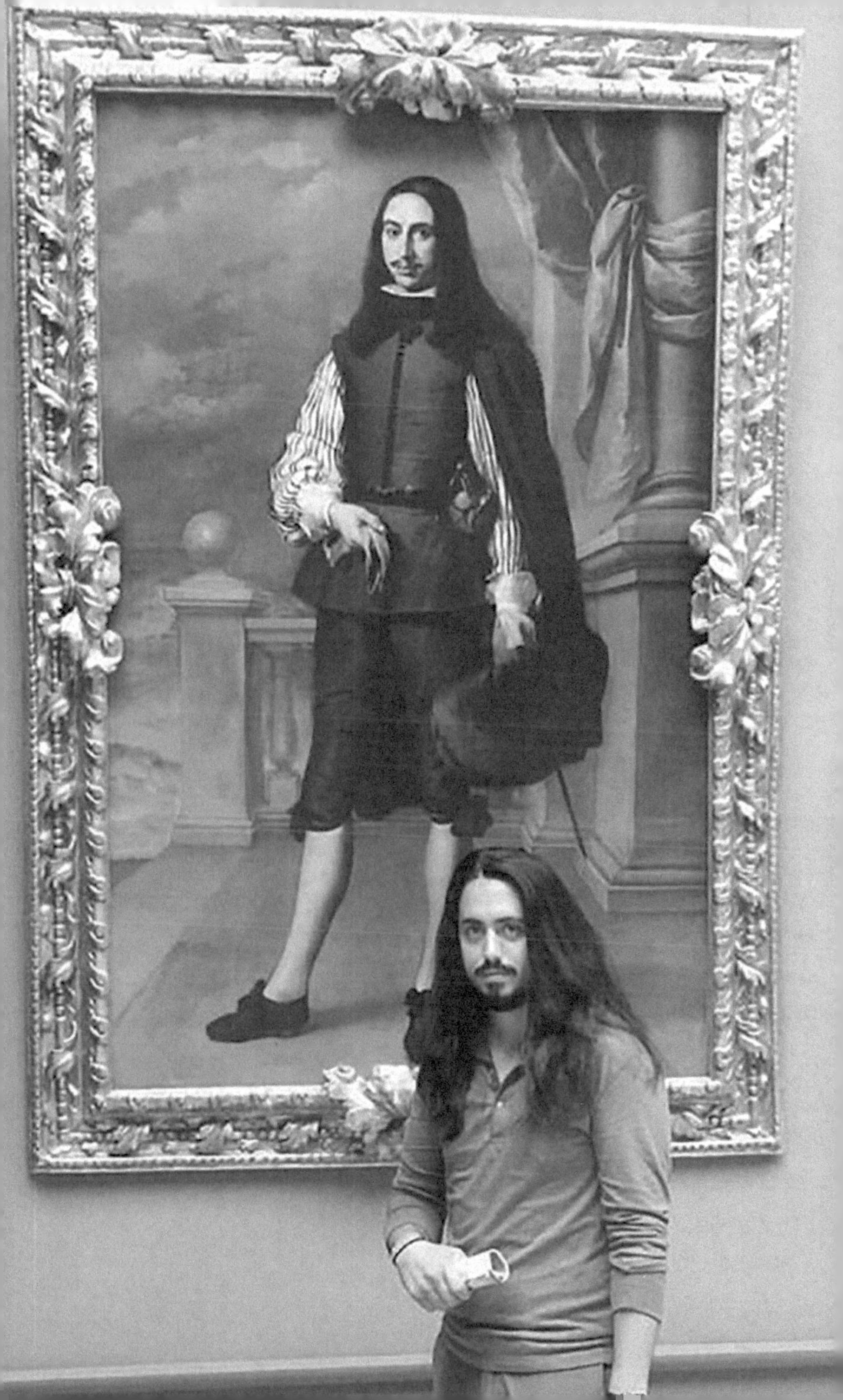

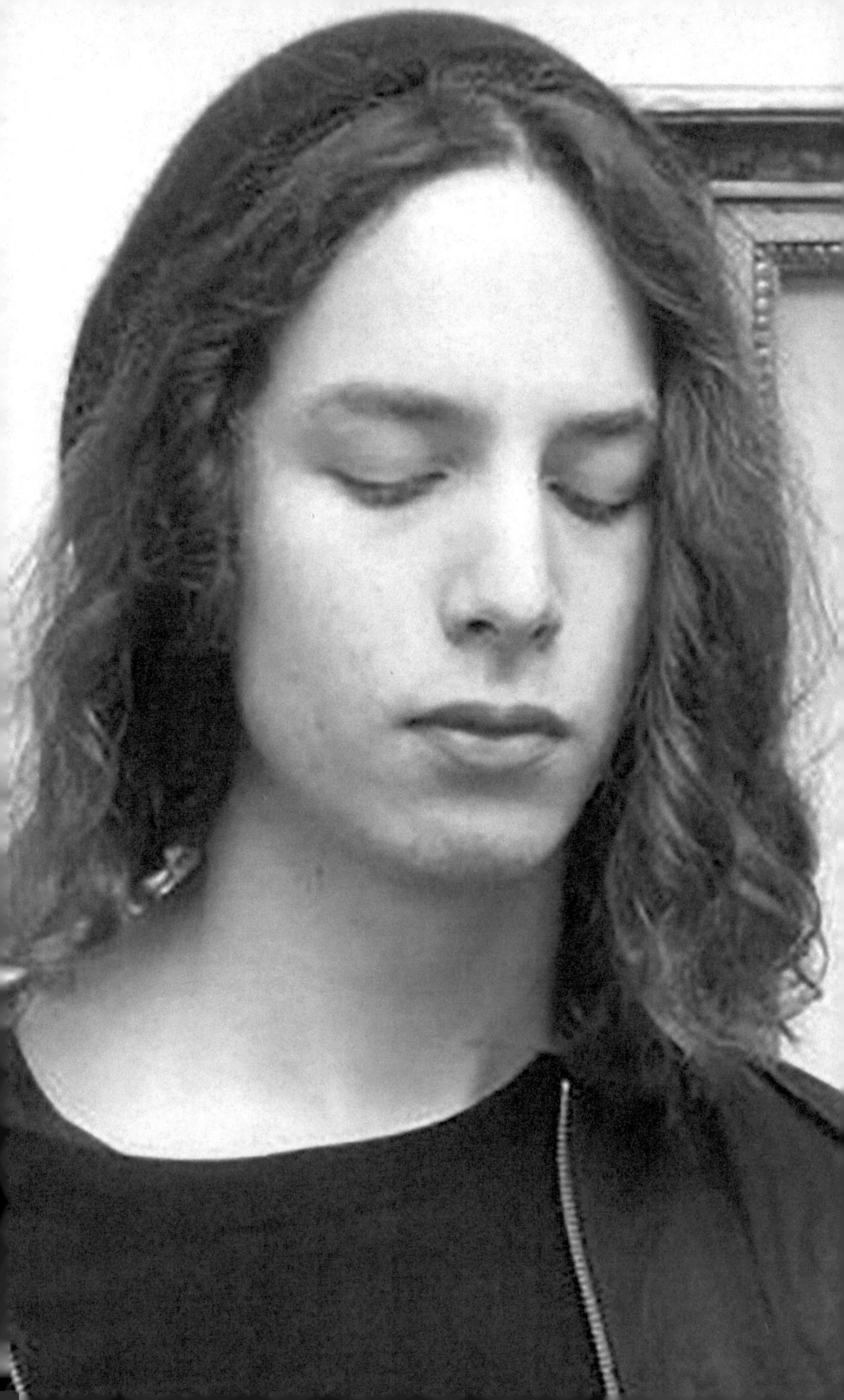

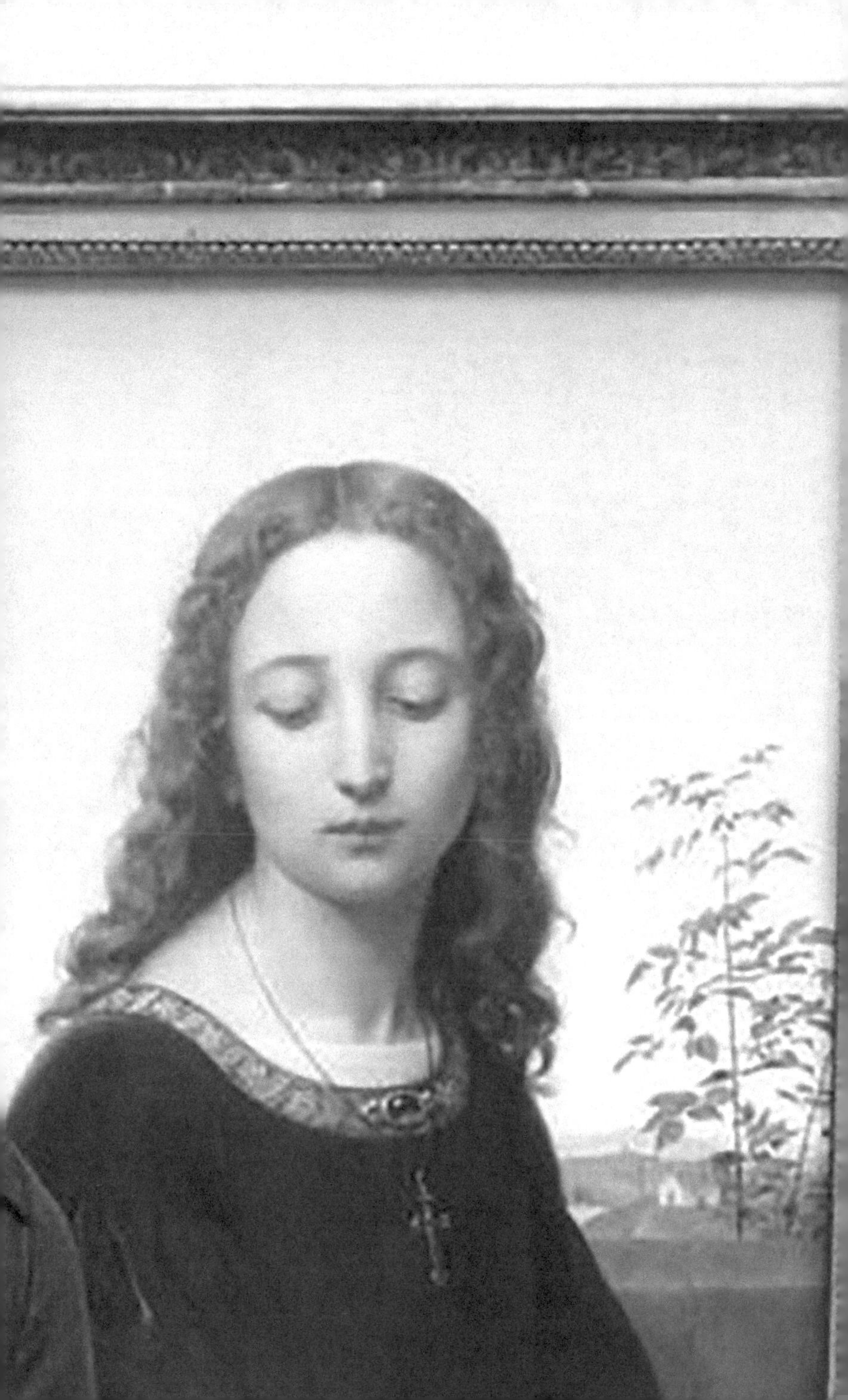

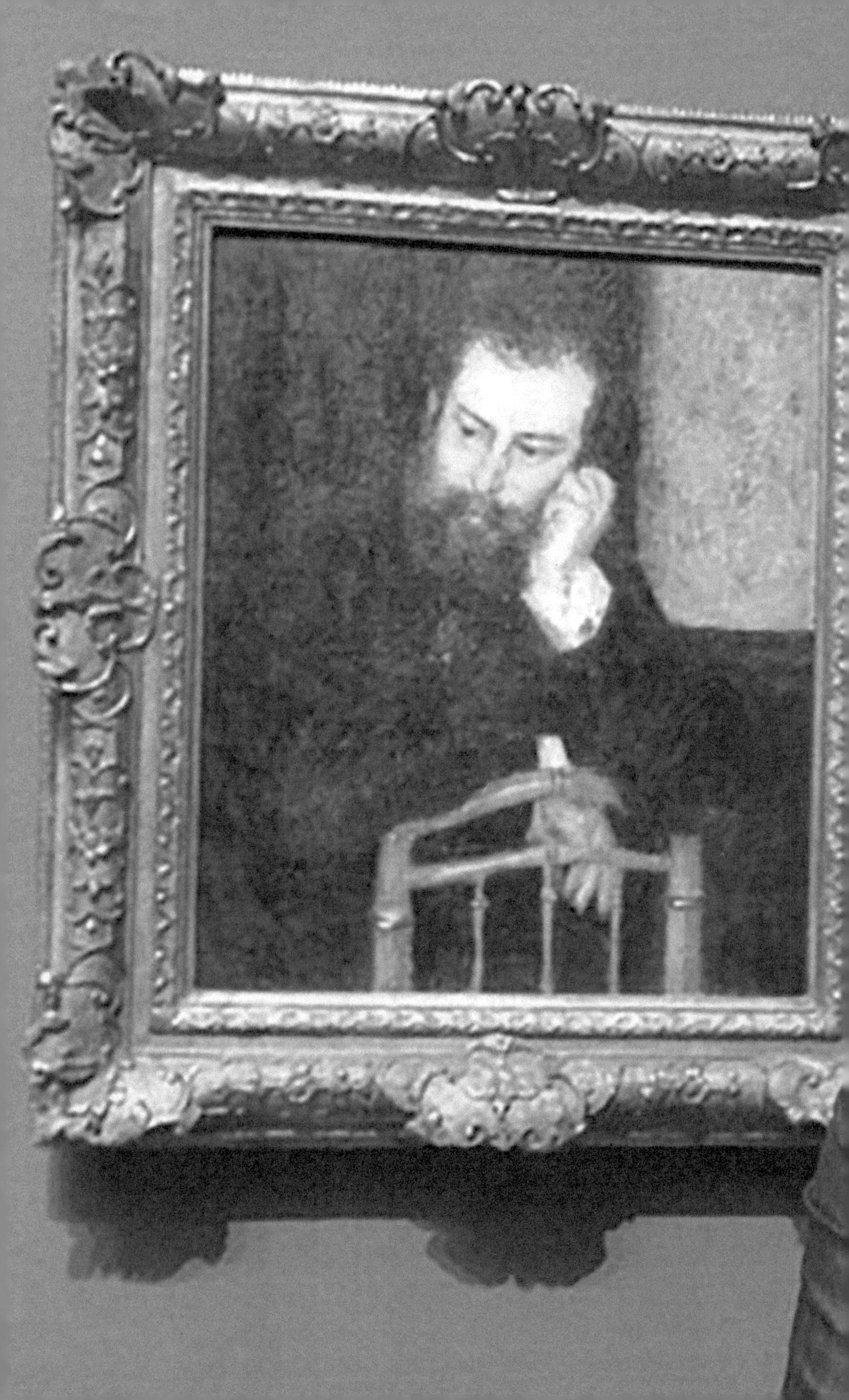

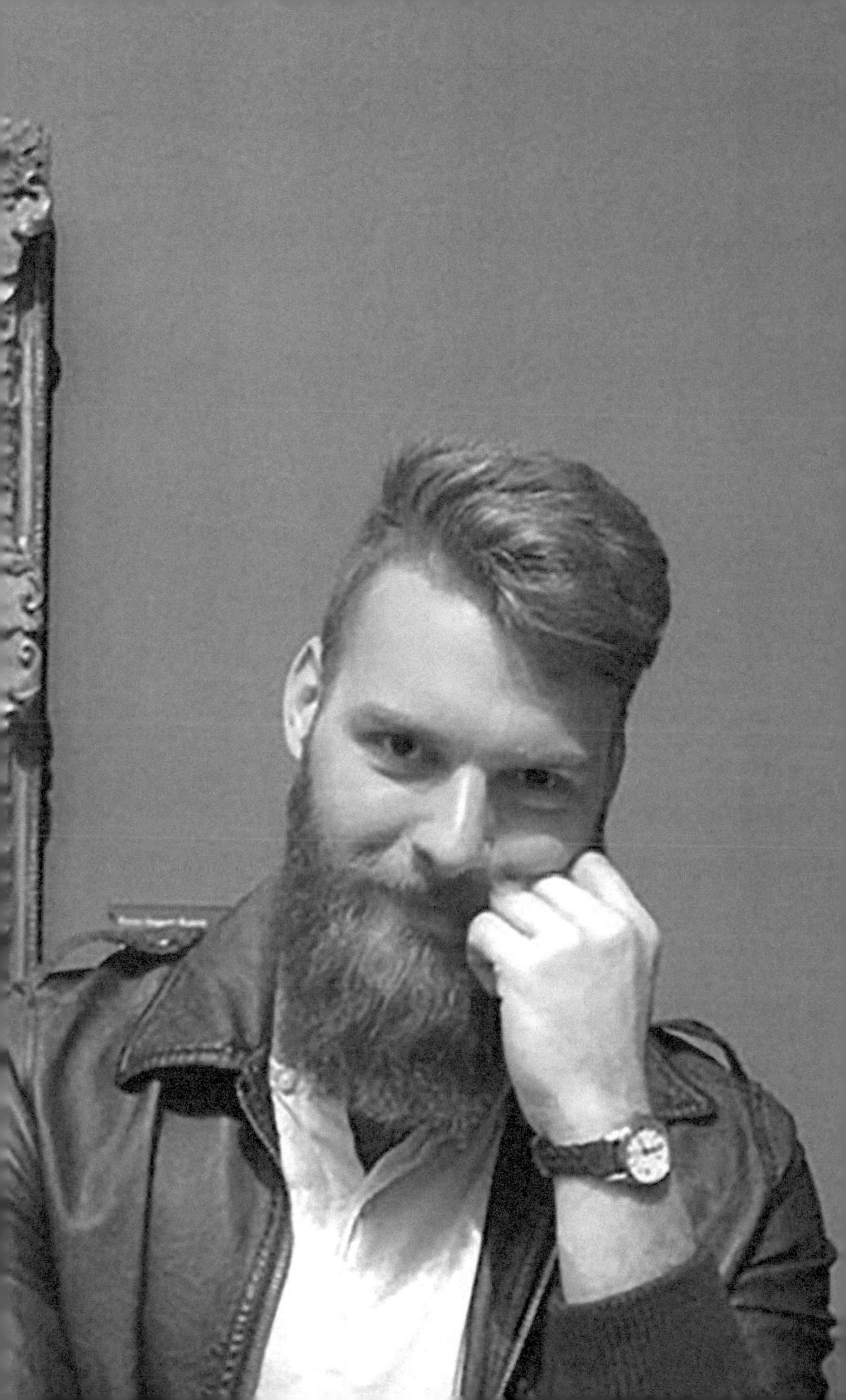

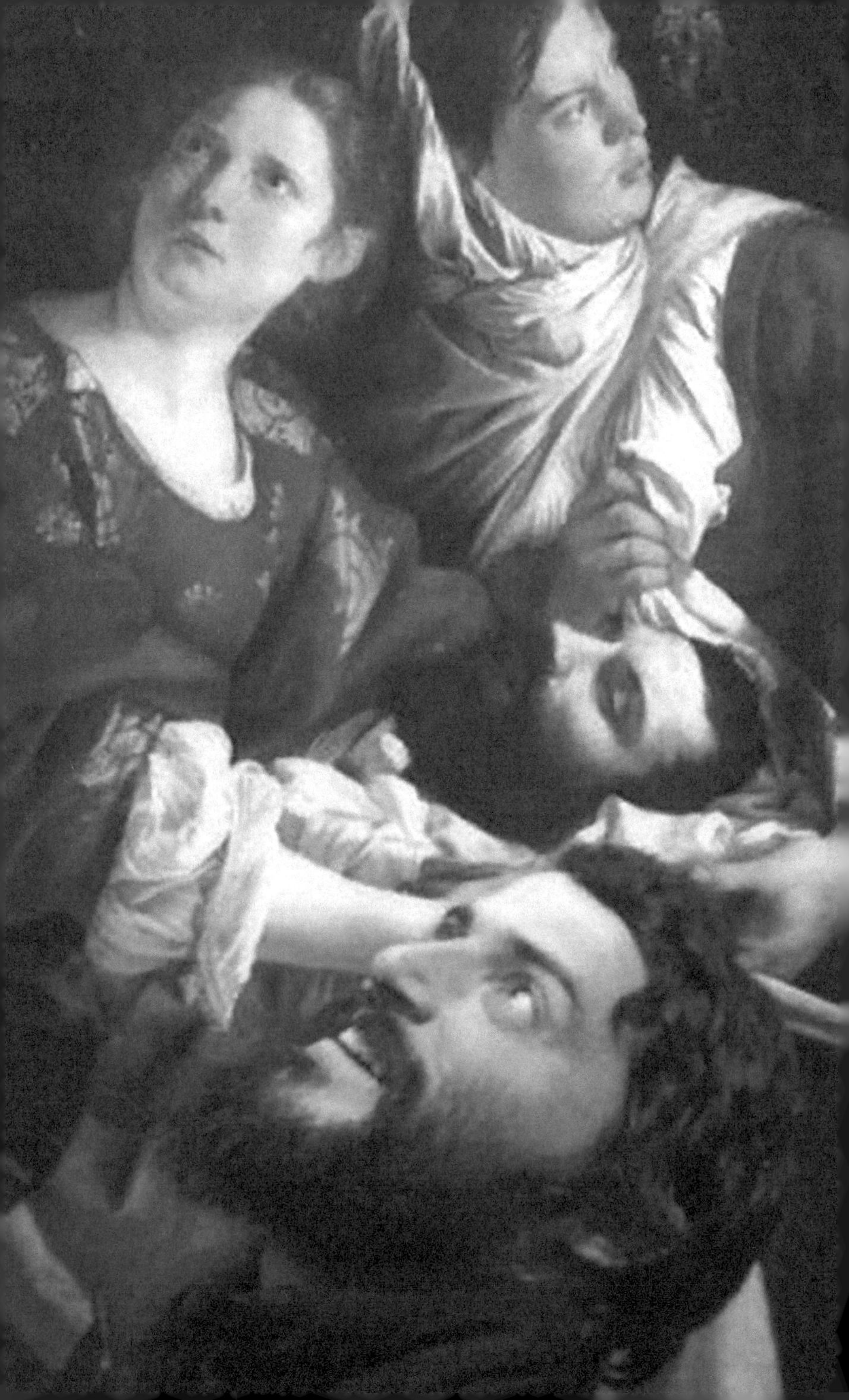

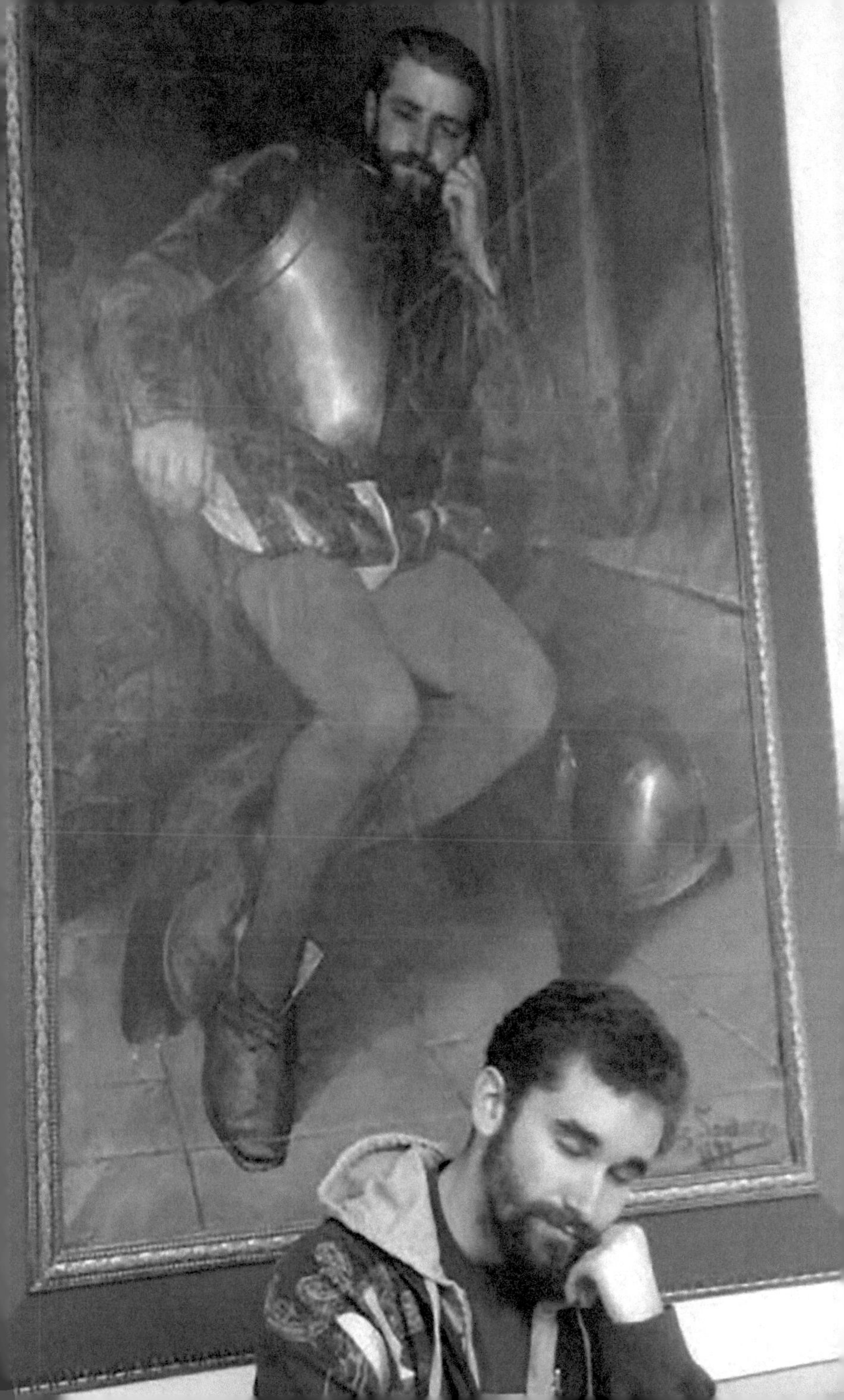

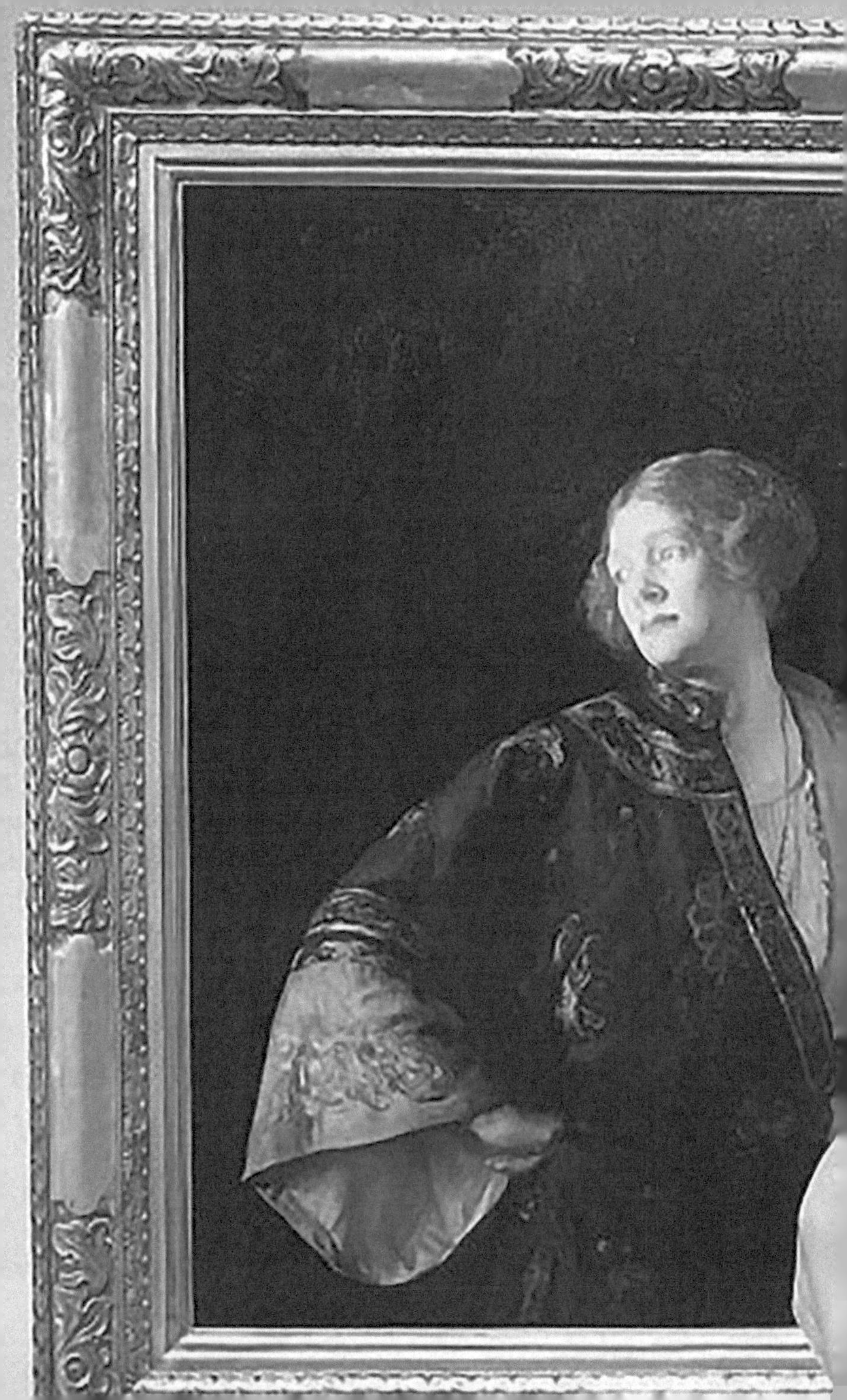

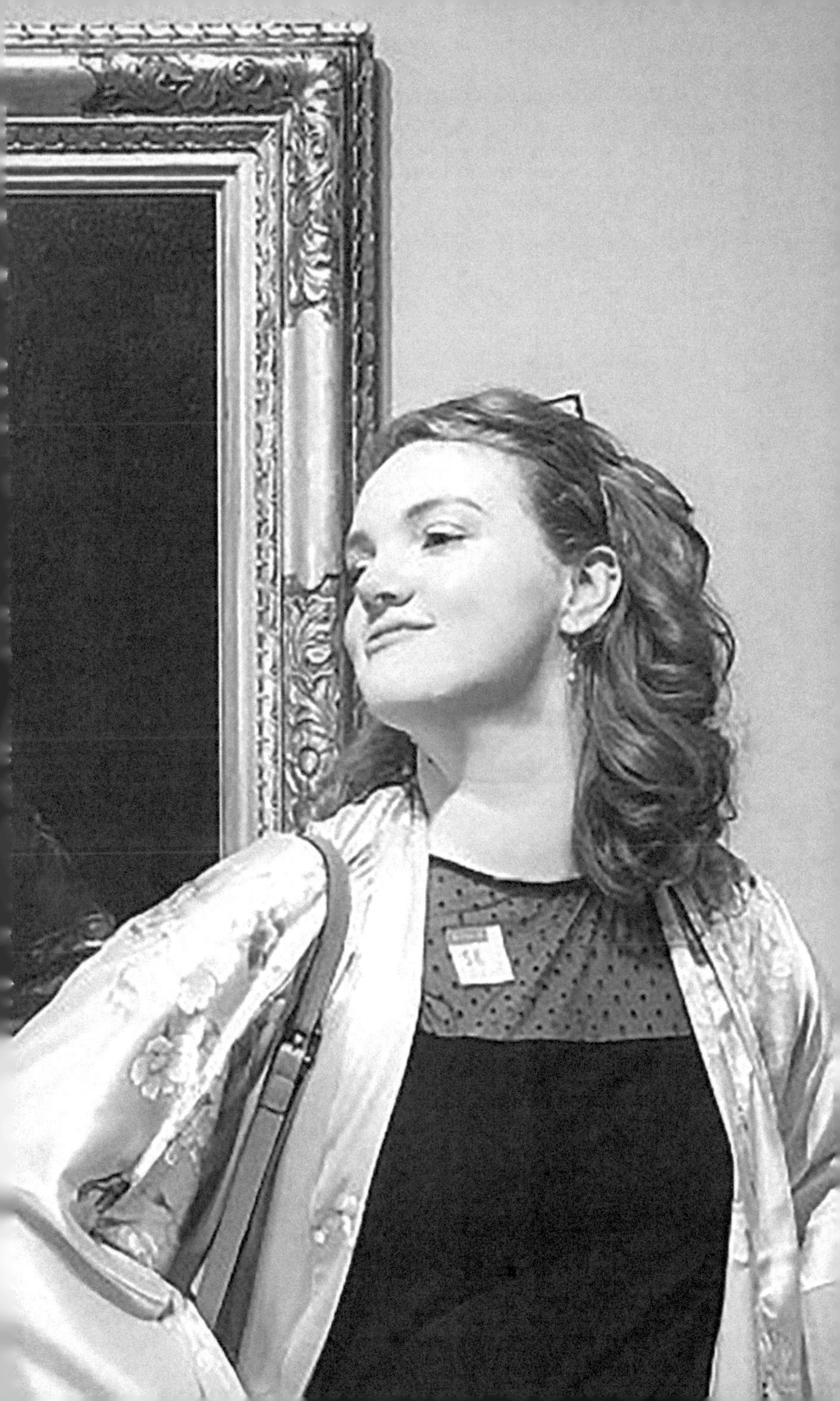

TIME TRAVELLERS
THOMAS MAILAENDER

THANKS TO ALL THE PHOTOGRAPHERS WHO LOVE PAINTINGS.

IMPRIMÉ EN FRANCE. ACHEVÉ D'IMPRIMER EN JUILLET 2022.
DÉPOT LÉGAL JUILLET 2022. ISBN 978-2-492175-15-2.
EDITION OF 200 COPIES

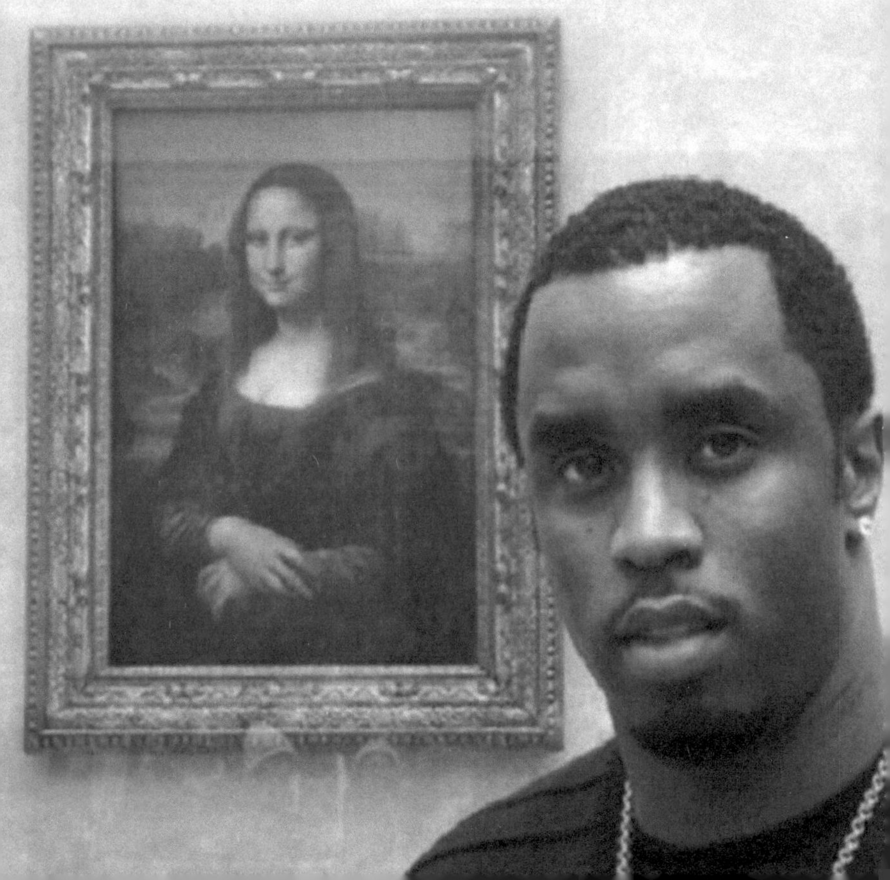